Baby Boomer Data: Hawai'i 2000

A Publication of the

Executive Office on Aging
State of Hawaii

No. 1 Capitol District
250 South Hotel Street - Suite 109
Honolulu, Hawai'i 96813-2831

Phone:808-586-0100
Fax:808-586-0185
e-mail:eoa@mail.health.state.hi.us
www.state.hi.us/health/eoa

This report was prepared by Harumi S. Karel, PhD, Kathryn L. Braun, DrPH, and Virginia M. Tanji, MSLS under contract with the Center on Aging, Office of Public Health Studies, John A. Burns School of Medicine, University of Hawaii.

This publication was funded by the Older Americans Act through the U. S. Administration on Aging and the Hawai'i State Legislature.

EXECUTIVE CHAMBERS
HONOLULU

BENJAMIN J. CAYETANO
GOVERNOR

MESSAGE FROM GOVERNOR BENJAMIN J. CAYETANO

December 4, 2000

I am pleased to present *Baby Boomer Data – Hawaii 2000*, a publication intended to increase our knowledge of the societal impact of the state's graying population. Hawaii has one of the highest growth rates of older persons in the nation, and it is important that we understand how this trend will influence our lives in the future.

The aging baby boomer population presents both government and our broader society with unprecedented challenges and opportunities. By the year 2020, twenty-five percent of all Hawaii residents will be at least sixty years of age, and many of our people will be living longer on average than ever before. As the baby boom evolves into the senior boom, we need to be prepared for the inevitable influences this demographic shift will have on such areas as economic development, health care, and delivery of critical social services.

This report presents a comprehensive look at a significant demographic trend confronting the state and its people. I hope you find it a welcome addition to the growing body of information on one of the important policy and planning issues of our time.

Aloha,

BENJAMIN J. CAYETANO

Our Logo

"E Loa Ke Ola"
May Life Be Long

Aloha and interdependence, a blend of Polynesian, Oriental and Western cultures…

…this is the visual message of the logo used by the Executive Office on Aging. The logo was created for and adopted by the Hawai'i State Commission on Aging in 1974. In 1977, the Executive Office on Aging replaced the Hawai'i State Commission on Aging.

The traditional Chinese ideograph for longevity translates, "The scholar struggles with his long hand continuously so that there will be food to feed every inch of his mouth."

Scholar-artist Hon-Chew Hee styled the Chinese character for longevity to create a Hawaiian petroglyph symbol which expresses Mary Kawena Pukui's translation of the Hawaiian words E LOA KE OLA – "May Life Be Long." The logo shows the family working together to "feed every inch of the mouth." The father of the family is depicted as tilling the land, while the mother is catching fish under water, and their son is spearing animals.

The expression of aging, island style, is a natural and welcome process with deep, joyous meaning to individuals and their families and communities. The logo symbolizes the desire of the people of Hawai'i to be blessed with long and fulfilling lives.

Table of Contents

EXECUTIVE SUMMARY

Background

Hawai`i's elderly population is growing, and is growing much faster than the nation as a whole. Consider:

- Residents 60 and older comprised 16% of our population in 1990. By 2020, the number of residents 60+ will have doubled over 1990, to represent 25% of the population.

- The population 65 and older (those eligible for Social Security and Medicare) will more than double in number. They comprised 11% of the total population in 1990, but will account for 18% in 2020. If military personnel and their dependents are excluded from the projections, the population 65 and older will account for 20% of the state's population in 2020.

- Residents 85 and older (those most in need of institutional, community, and in-home services due to high levels of disability, both mental and physical) comprised 1% of our total population in 1990. By 2020, the number of residents 85+ will have more than tripled, to represent 2.6% of the total population.

Why is the elderly population growing so quickly? Much of the growth is due to the aging of the baby boomers, the massive population blip attributable to high birth rates from 1946 through 1964 In fact:

- By 2011, the first boomers will reach the conventional retirement age of 65.

- By 2030, all baby boomers will be 65 years old and older.

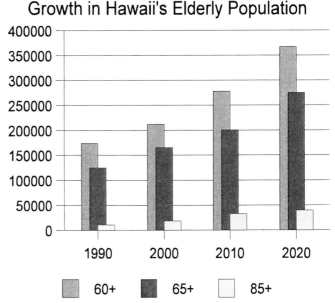

Growth in Hawaii's Elderly Population

The societal impact of graying baby boomers has been the subject of speculation and debate by U.S. policy makers, economists, and other professionals. Reasons why the aging boomer population is a major concern include: 1) the swiftness of the increase of the population; 2) the prolonged life expectancy resulting in a prolonged duration of "old age;" 3) current changes in family structures and the impact of these changes on the ability of families to care for their older members; and 4) changing notions about social and public responsibility for supporting this increasing number of older Americans.

In general, the U.S. baby boomer cohort is thought to have a higher standard of living than the previous generations. Boomers have altered traditional family structures by marrying late and having fewer children, and frequently ending marriages and entering into new relationships. They are also thought to spend more money than they save.

As the "baby boom" turns into the "senior boom," Hawai`i policy makers may want to consider these questions:

- What is a typical baby boomer in Hawai`i?

- How do Hawai`i's baby boomers compare to the previous generation (i.e., Hawai`i's current seniors citizens)? How do they compare with U.S. baby boomers as a whole?

- What else do we know about baby boomers that can give us some ideas about their future needs and desires?

- When Hawai`i's boomers are senior citizens, what demands will they place on government?

To begin to answer these questions, this report presents a compilation of current and projected data about Hawai`i's baby boomers. Their characteristics are compared with those of their parents' generation and with those of baby boomers in the U.S. as a whole. The report then speculates about what types of assistance baby boomers may need when they enter "old age."

Findings

What is a typical baby boomer in Hawai`i? Existing data from a number of federal and state sources suggest that:

> *The typical boomer in Hawai`i is an Asian or Pacific Islander and a high school graduate (only 27% are college graduates). He/she most likely lives in a family household, having married at around age 30. He/she has a job and his/her family income is about $40,000. The typical boomer wears seatbelts, does not smoke or drink, and is not overweight. If this boomer were to die, he/she would be likely to die from cancer, heart disease, or injury. But the majority of boomers can expect to live another 25 to 45 years. He/she does not own a home (only 41% do). His/her parents are still living, and the boomer may expect to inherit property or income from them.*

> *Although there is no specific data available for Hawai`i boomers, national data suggest that our typical boomer is not saving regularly for retirement (only 42% are) and is not participating in a pension plan (only 44% are).*

How do Hawai`i's baby boomers compare to the previous generation (i.e., Hawai`i's current seniors citizens)? How do they compare with U.S. baby boomers as a whole? Existing data from a number of federal and state sources suggest Hawai`i baby boomers:

- will live longer than today's senior citizens,
- have more formal education than today's senior citizens,
- have higher median family and household incomes than today's senior citizens (although the cost of living is much higher today than it was 20-40 years ago),
- have fewer children than their parents' generation,
- have higher rates of divorce and remarriage than their parents' generation,
- if female, are more likely to participate in the labor force than their mothers,
- are less likely to own a home than their parents, and
- are much more likely to smoke, drink, and be overweight than their parents' generation.

In Comparison to U.S. Boomers as a whole, Hawai`i baby boomers:

- will live longer than mainland boomers,
- have more formal education than mainland boomers,
- have fewer children than mainland boomers,
- have higher rates of divorce and remarriage than mainland boomers,
- have a higher median family income than boomers on the mainland (although the cost of living in Hawai`i is higher than on the mainland),
- if female, are more likely to participate in the labor force than female boomers on the mainland,
- are less likely to own their own home than boomers on the mainland, and
- are less likely to smoke, more likely to drink, and more likely to use seatbelts than mainland boomers.

As far as their retirement plan is concerned, many boomers are not saving for retirement. A survey by the American Association for Retired People (AARP) found that only 42% reported saving regularly for retirement and that boomers did not have a large store of assets. Excluding house equity, leading-edge boomers (those born 1946-1955) had only $18,000 in assets while trailing-edge boomers (those born 1956-1964) had only $7,000 in assets. According to Merrill Lynch, the retirement saving adequacy of baby boomers (all households) in 1996 was 35.9%, suggesting that baby boomers need to save three times more for retirement than they're now saving (Bernheim, 1997).

Baby boomers report in a number of surveys that they expect Medicare and Medicaid will cover their health and long-term care costs as they age. In fact, U.S. health care costs for adults 65+ are projected to increase from $31 billion in 1994 to $665 billion in 2030, an increase of over 2000%. In Hawai`i, long-term care costs, including costs of nursing homes and home care services, will increase from $181 million in 1990 to $2,050 million in 2020, an increase of over 1000%. Can public insurance programs cover all these costs? Don't people have private insurance? Surprisingly, it is projected that less than 10% of Hawai`i's population will have private long-term care insurance by 2020. Mainland studies have found that long-term care insurance is the payer for only 1% of long-term care costs.

Hawai`i's baby boomers will face added burden due to the higher <u>dependency ratio</u> than the mainland. The dependency ratio is the ratio of adults 65+ to working-age adults. Hawai`i's dependency ratio will increase from 21.5 older adults per 100 working-age adults in 1995 to 30 older adults to100 working-age adults in 2020. Thus, Hawai`i will have a shrinking number of working-age adults (who contribute to the tax base) trying to support a growing number of adults 65+ (who use many of the services supported by state and federal taxes).

In addition, Hawai`i's <u>parent's support ratio</u> (the ratio of adults 85+ per adults 50-64, who are most likely to be family caregivers) will increase from 8.7 adults 85+ per 100 family caregivers in 1995 to 15.7 adults 85+ per 100 family caregivers in 2020. Thus, Hawai`i will have a shrinking number of middle-aged adults trying to support a growing number of adults 85+ (who are most likely to be disabled, frail, or vulnerable).

Implications for Government

The data presented in this report suggest that Hawai`i state government will need to consider new ways of delivering and financing services as "baby boomers" become "senior boomers." Given the expected diversity among the 18-year cohort of boomers, implications are discussed for two groups of aged boomers: 1) those who are healthy and active and 2) those who are disabled, frail, or vulnerable.

- Healthy and Active Aged "Senior Boomers"

Hawai`i baby boomers are less likely to accept the status quo and are used to having more independence than their parent's generation. Upon retirement, we can expect these boomers to continue to exercise their freedom of choice and to demand goods and services they believe are due to them. This group of seniors will present challenges and opportunities to a number of areas of government responsibility and concern:

  - Labor and Industry
  - Transportation
  - Taxation
  - Education
  - Leisure Activities

- Disabled, Frail, and Vulnerable "Senior Boomers"

Hawai`i baby boomers are generally in good health and will live longer than their parent's generation, but greater proportions smoke, drink, and are overweight than the current generation of elders. They have smaller and more-scattered families, and many do not own homes. There is a growing segment that are not saving for retirement while, at the same time, the dependence ratio is increasing (meaning that fewer young people are available to work and contribute to the tax base that supports income-maintenance, health, and social service programs). Thus the number of elders who are disabled, frail, and vulnerable will increase as the number of family and tax-dependent supports

4

decreases. This group of seniors will present challenges to a number of areas of government responsibility and concern:

- Income Maintenance
- Transportation
- Housing
- Consumer Protection
- Prisons
- Health and Social Services
- Long-Term Care

PART I
INTRODUCTION

Background

The baby boom cohort consists of Americans born between 1946 and 1964. Currently, the U.S. counts 83 million baby boomers, representing about one-third of the population. Of these, about 75 million were born in the U.S. and about 8 million were foreign-born.

The rapid growth of the elderly population, which will surge when the baby boomers begin to enter "old age" in the year 2011, has become a major concern among U.S. policy makers, economists, and health professionals.

In 1990, the elderly population in the U.S. (those 65 and older) included 31 million people and accounted for about 12.5% of the total population. By the year 2030, when all the baby boomers will be 65 and older, the number is projected to be 70 million, more than double the 1990 figure (www.aoa.dhhs.gov, 1996).

In Hawai`i, only 11.3% of the population was 65 and older in 1990. But Hawai`i's proportion of older adults is increasing much faster than in other states; by 2020, 21% of Hawai`i residents will be 65 and older, compared to only 16% in the U.S. as a whole. Even more startling, by 2020, 25% of residents, one in every four, will be 60 and older (DBEDT, 1996).

Reasons why the aging boomer population is a major concern include (Cornman, 1997):

- The swiftness of the increase of the population

- The prolonged life expectancy resulting in a prolonged duration of "old age"

- Current changes in family structures and the impact of these changes on the ability of the family to care for its older members

- Changing notions about social and public responsibility for supporting this increasing number of older Americans

The baby boomers have been, and continue to be, the most-studied cohort in the United States. Compared to the preceding generations, baby boomers seem different in a number of ways. A major reason for these differences was the contraceptive revolution. With wide access to birth control, baby boomers have set new norms in fertility patterns, redefined the concept of family, created new types of households and living options, allowed more women into the workplace, and renegotiated gender roles (Wattenberg, 1986).

In addition, baby boomers grew up in relative affluence compared to the preceding generation. Although many engaged in anti-materialistic and counter-cultural activities of the Vietnam era, many now seem to be driven to acquire and maintain a highly visible consumer-oriented lifestyle -- a transformation from "hippies" to "yuppies."

A review of the baby boomer literature acknowledges continuing gaps between genders and among ethnic groups. However, scholars have suggested a number of commonly understood characteristics of baby boomers (Cornman & Kingson, 1996; Easterline et al., 1990; Fullerton, 1991; Lumsdon, 1993; Macunovich et al., 1995; Manton & Stallard, 1996; Vincenzino, 1996). Baby boomers:

- are the most highly educated generation in American history.

- tended to marry later in life, end marriages more frequently, delay childbearing, and have fewer children than previous generations.

- have altered traditional family structures and living arrangements, with an increased prevalence of one-parent and non-traditional families.

- are, on average, financially better off than their parents' generation.

- tend to be spenders rather than savers. Thus, despite educational and economic advantages, the economic prospects of baby boomers, when they enter old age, are thought to be poor.

- are extremely mobile, distrustful of institutions, and relatively self-centered.

- are keen to acquire information to manage their illnesses and avoid future risks and complications. They are attracted to products and services that promote "youthful and healthy aging," and not adverse to exploring alternative medicines and therapies.

- are less satisfied with current health care services compared to previous cohorts, and refuse to accept advice at face value. They tend to be among the most demanding patients in any treatment setting, asking for quality, expertise, excellent services, and convenience.

Some researchers are pessimistic about the future for baby boomers. Many worry that unless diagnostic and treatment advances are realized quickly, there will be a pandemic of chronic diseases and mass dementia. Others worry that baby boomers will not only face financial insecurity themselves when they enter "old age," but also face a caregiving crunch while they try to care for both their children and their parents, and maybe even their grandparents (Bouvier & De Vita, 1991; Dychtwald, 1997; Callahan, 1994; Singer & Manton, 1998).

Other researchers, however, are quite optimistic about the future. Despite poor savings habits, some analysts feel that the baby boomers will survive economically because they have deferred marriage, reduced the number of children they have, and benefitted from the increased labor force participation of wives (Easterline, 1990). In addition, the future of baby boomers' health may not be as catastrophic as predicted by some researchers due to continual advances in medical technology. In fact, there is some indication that disability and incidence of Alzheimer's disease are already on the decline (Blanchette & Valcour, 1998).

Purpose and Organization of this Report

The purpose of this report is to examine the characteristics of baby boomers in Hawai`i, to compare Hawai`i's boomers against commonly held notions, to speculate about the future of boomers as "elders," and to explore some of the implications for Hawai`i state government.

This report is organized in five major parts:

- Part I   Introduction
- Part II   Methods
- Part III   Current and Future Characteristics of Baby Boomers
- Part IV   Discussion
- Part V   Technical Appendix

Part III, Current and Future Characteristics of Baby Boomers, includes bullet points of information, along with illustrative charts and graphs. The bullet points are organized as follows:

- The first bullets present data comparing the boomers in Hawai`i with the 1990 census data.
- The middle bullets provide any updated information about the Hawai`i boomers, along with county data if available.
- The final bullets present projections about graying boomers. If projections about Hawai`i boomers are not available, general projections are included.

Part V, the Technical Appendix, includes the actual numbers upon which the narrative is based, and these are in the form of detailed tables.

It is hoped that this report will assist decision makers, policy makers, and other professionals to gain insights about the baby boomer cohort, its impact on the future demography of Hawai`i, and the influence of this demography on future health, social, and economic needs of the state.

Part II
Method

Sources of Information

Information and the data for the report were gathered from various sources, including journal articles, government documents, monographs, data books, and Web sites. In addition, the report includes data from a special analysis conducted by the Hawai`i Department of Health and secondary analysis of census data using the Ferret system at the U.S. Bureau of Census web site. No new data were collected for this report.

Limitations

This method presents a number of challenges to researchers. For example, different sources report data in different categories for different purposes, hindering cross-source comparisons. Challenges specifically encountered in preparing this report are reviewed here.

First, the term "baby boomer" is a socially constructed concept that refers to Americans born between 1946 and 1964, a span of 18 years. Although members of this group experienced many of the same political, economic, and social events of the past several decades, they experienced them at different time points. In fact, some researchers differentiate between leading-edge boomers (those born between 1946-1955) and trailing-edge baby boomers (those born between 1956-1964). It is suggested that leading-edge baby boomers had more advantages than the trailing-edge baby boomers, for example better access to jobs, public and privately funded services, and pensions (Bouvier & De Vita, 1991; Leventhal, 1994). Individual boomers' experiences differed as well by the region of the country they lived in, whether they were U.S.-born or foreign-born, and personal health habits and family events. It can only be expected, then, that individual baby boomers will differ in their needs, expectations, and preparedness in "old age."

Available resource documents differed in their definitions of various age groups. For example, the 1990 Census defined baby boomers as those age 26-44 whereas other reports said that the boomers were age 25-44 in 1990. When referring to baby boomers as a proportion of the whole population, this one-year difference in definition is not problematic. But when trying to specify the actual number of baby boomers, the one-year difference in definition is significant.

Similarly, the starting point for "old age" is not consistent across reports. For example, Social Security uses "65 and older," the Older Americans Act uses "60 and older," and the American Association of Retired Persons offers full benefits to members "50 and older." The "old-old" age category is also elusive, sometimes referred to as "80 and older" and other times as "85 and older." Inconsistent use of age cut-off points greatly complicates cross-source comparisons.

Population projections also varied depending on the institution presenting the information. Usually, three population projections are calculated--a low-range projection, middle-range projection, and high-range projection. For this report, the middle-range projections were used.

We also found minor inconsistencies in population counts, even from the same source (e.g., sometimes an agency's printed report contained numbers slightly different from those posted on its Web site). For example, according to the U.S. Census Bureau's web site, the number of baby boomers in Hawai`i in 1990 was 358,653, where other census information stated 379,035 and the information from DBEDT indicated 361,859.

Some agencies offer projections to the year 2030 (when all baby boomers will be 65 or older) and 2050 (when surviving baby boomers will be 85 or older), but others only offer projections to the year 2010 or 2020.

Because of these differences, actual findings and projections from one source may differ from another. Readers can still draw general conclusions, as data presented are from reputable studies that examined valid data sources.

Finally, readers should bear in mind that predictions about the future are based on current trends. The future, however, is affected by much more than numbers. Political decisions and policy changes will alter the future for baby boomers considerably. As policy changes, so will trends, and so will our possible futures.

Abbreviations

AARP	American Association of Retired Persons (national non-profit organization)
AoA	Administration on Aging (federal agency)
BOC	Bureau of the Census (federal agency)
BRFSS	Behavioral Risk Factor Surveillance System (federally supported data collection system conducted by states)
CDC	Centers for Disease Control and Prevention (federal agency)
DBEDT	Department of Business, Economic Development, and Tourism (Hawai`i agency)
DLIR	Department of Labor and Industrial Relations (Hawai`i agency)
DOH	Department of Health (Hawai`i agency)
EBRI	Employee Benefit Research Institute
EOA	Executive Office on Aging (Hawai`i agency)
HMSA	Hawai`i Medical Service Association (non-profit)
HCFA	Health Care Financing Administration (federal agency)

PART III
CURRENT AND FUTURE CHARACTERISTICS
OF BABY BOOMERS IN HAWAI`I

Demographic And Social Characteristics

Population

The proportion of older adults has been increasing over the last decades in the United States. However, the cohort of baby boomers begins to enter the "old age" category in 2011, both the number and proportion of older adults will increase dramatically. By 2020, Hawai`i residents 60 and older will represent 25% of the state's population, that's one out of every four people (Figure 1). The detailed population projection is depicted in Table 1 in Part II of this report.

- In 1990, the baby boomers (born between 1946-1964, age 26-44) represented 32.5% of total population in Hawai`i, while adults 60 and older (born 1930 or before) represented 11.3%. By 1998, the baby boomers represented 29.7% and adults 60+ represented 17% of the total population. (www.census.gov,1996-a; www.state.hi.us/dbedt, 1998).

- In 1998, the leading-edge baby boomers (those born between 1946-1955) represented 49.2% of total baby boomers while the trailing-edge baby boomers (those born between 1956-1964) represented 50.8% of all boomers. (Table 2)

- In 1998, almost 32% of Maui County's population were boomers, compared to 29% of O`ahu's population, 30% of Hawai`i County's population, and 30% of Kaua`i County's population. (Table 2)

- Overall, Hawai`i, Maui, and Kaua`i Counties are projected to have higher population-growth rates than Honolulu City and County between now and 2020. Neighbor Island counties will grow 1.5% annually compared to 0.8% annual growth projected for O`ahu. (DBEDT, 1997)

- The median age of people in Hawai`i will rise from 34.5 in 1995 to 37.3 in 2020. However, when the military personnel and their dependents are excluded from the projection, the median age will be almost 40 years in 2020. (DBEDT, 1996)

- In the U.S., the population 60 and older is projected to increase from 16.6% in 1995 to 22.9% in 2020. Hawai`i's 60+ population will grow the fastest of all states, from 16.4% in 1995 to 24.6% in 2020. (Figure 1, Table 3)

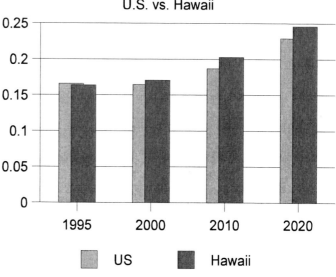

Figure 1: Projection of Elderly Age 60+: 1995-2020 U.S. vs. Hawaii

- In 1990, the 65+ population represented 11.3% of Hawai`i's total population, compared to 12.5% for the U.S. as a whole. When the leading-edge Hawai`i baby boomers begin to enter "old age" in 2011, the 65+ population will represent 16% of the state's population, increasing to 18% in 2020. In the U.S. as a whole, however, those 65+ will represent only 13% of the total population in 2010, and 16% in 2020. When the military personnel and their dependents are excluded from Hawai`i's projection, people 65+ will represent 20% of the total population in 2020. (Figure 2, Table 4)

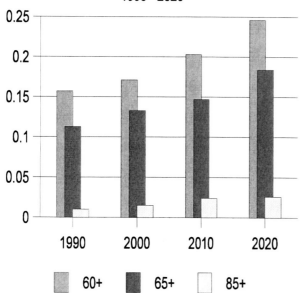

Figure 2: Projection of Elderly in Hawaii 1990 - 2020

- In 1995, the "old-old" (those 80 and older) constituted 24% of Americans 65 and older. In Hawai`i, 21% of our elders were 80+ in 1995. By 2010, however, there will be a significant increase of "old-old," when those 80+ will constitute 32% of our elderly population. When the leading-edge baby boomers enter "old age" (2011-2021) the proportion of "young-old" (those between 65-79) will increase and the proportion of our elderly who are in the "old-old" category will decrease. However, the proportion of "old-old" elderly is expected to increase again when the leading-edge baby boomers reach their 80s, starting in 2020. (Table 5)

12

Life Expectancy

For Americans as a whole, life expectancy has increased tremendously over the past century. This is true for both life expectancy at birth and life expectancy at age 65. In 1900, life expectancy of Americans at birth was 47 years, while life expectancy in 1990 was 75 years. Life expectancy is projected to increase to 81.8 for females and 76.2 for males by 2030. Currently, the life expectancy of people in Hawai`i (79 years) is among the highest in the United States. If the current situation continues, people in Hawai`i will live longer than their U.S. counterparts.

- In 1990, the life expectancy at birth in Hawai`i was 79. For the U.S. as a whole, the life expectancy at birth was 75. (Table 6)

- By gender, the life expectancy at birth in Hawai`i in 1990 was 82 for females and 76 for males. For the U.S. as a whole, life expectancy at birth was 79 for females and 72 for males. (Table 6)

- In 1990, Chinese in Hawai`i had the longest life expectancy at birth--83 years--followed by Japanese--82 years. When the baby boomers were born in the 1940s and 1950s, Japanese had the longest life expectancy at birth (almost 73 in 1950) compared to Caucasian, Chinese, and Filipinos (69-70 years). Hawaiians had the lowest life expectancy at birth in 1990--74 years–and have had the lowest life expectancy for much of the century. (Table 7)

- At age 65, the U.S. Bureau of the Census projects that life expectancy is another 22 years for females and another 20 years for males. (Figure 3, Table 8)

- If the current trends continue, people in Hawai`i can generally expect to live 3 to 4 years longer than people on the mainland.

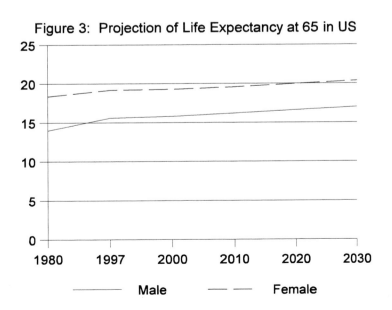

Figure 3: Projection of Life Expectancy at 65 in US

Gender

Since life expectancy for females is much longer than for males, and since male mortality is usually higher than female mortality at all ages, women generally outnumber men. However, male boomers in Hawai`i outnumbered female boomers in 1990. By 1998, the gender distribution among Hawai`i boomers reached parity with the U.S. By 2020, Hawai`i can expect 82.5 males per 100 females in the 65+ population but only 59.8 males per 100 females in the 85+ population.

- In the U.S., the proportion of female baby boomers was 50.3% in 1990. In Hawai`i, however, only 48.6% of boomers were female. (www.census.gov, 1996-a)

- In 1998, gender distribution for boomers in Hawai`i reached parity with the U.S., with males comprising 50.7% of boomers and females comprising 49.3% of boomers. (www.census.gov, 1998)

- In the U.S., the ratio of males to females among adults 65+ was 68.9 males per 100 females in 1995. In 2030, it will increase to 84.2 males per 100 females in the 65+ age group. For adults age 85+, however, there will be only 55.6 males per 100 females in 2030. (www.aoa.dhhs.gov, 1996-b).

- In Hawai`i, the ratio of males to females for adults 65+ was 85.9 males per 100 females in 1995 and it is projected to be 82.5 males per 100 females in 2020. For adult 85+, however, there will be 59.8 per 100 females in 2020 (Figure 4, Table 9).

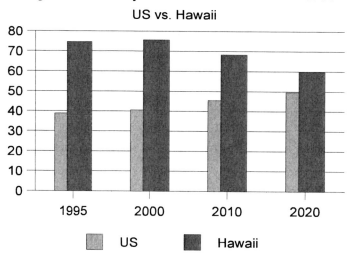

Figure 4: The Projection of Sex Ratio of Adults 85+ US vs. Hawaii

Racial and Ethnic Diversity

Hawai`i has one of the largest concentrations of Asian and Pacific Islanders and one of the highest rates of foreign immigration among the 50 states (DBEDT, 1996). Immigration plays an important role in changing the size and the diversity of minority populations. Although Japanese have comprised the largest ethnic minority group in Hawai`i, the Filipino population will rapidly increase in the future due to their relatively high rates of fertility and immigration.

- In Hawai`i, 57% of baby boomers were of a "minority" ethnic group, mostly Asian and Pacific Islanders, in 1990. For the U.S. as a whole, only 3.3% of boomers were of a "minority"ethnic group. (Figure 5, Table 10)

- More specifically, the 1990 ethnic distribution of the baby boomers in Hawai`i (per the U.S. Census) was White (38.4%), Japanese (20.0%), Filipino (13.8%), Hawaiian (10.7%), Chinese (6.1%), other Pacific Islanders (3.7%), Black (2.9%), Korean (2.4%), and other (2.0%). (Figure 6, Table 11)

- The majority of Black baby boomers were living in Honolulu County. This was due largely to a concentration of military personnel on the island of O`ahu. (Table 12)

- Maui County had the largest percentage of boomers who were White (47%), followed by Hawai`i (46%), Kaua`i (42%), and Honolulu (36%). (Table 12)

- In 1990, 45.8% of baby boomers living in Hawai`i were foreign-born, compared to 38% for the U.S. as a whole. Hawai`i had a large percentage of people who immigrated or migrated from overseas (www.census.gov, 1996-a).

Figure 5: Racial Composition of Baby Boomers: U.S. vs. Hawaii
In 1990 (Perentage)

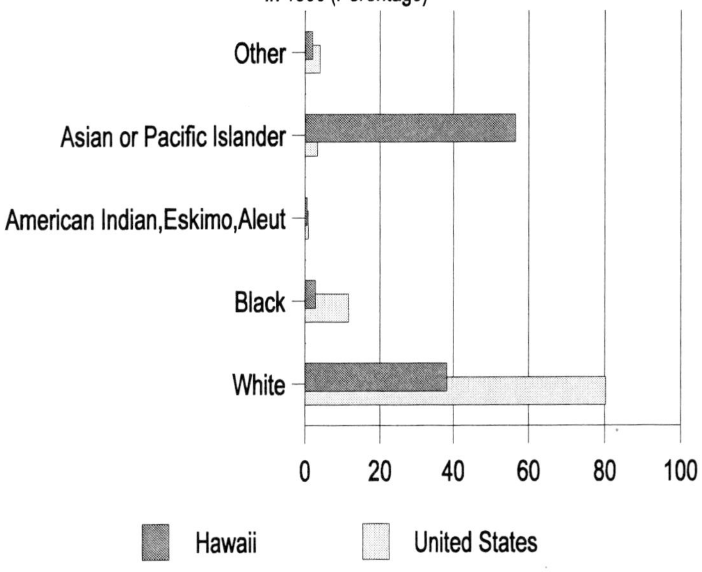

- In 1990, 74% of Hawai`i residents 60 and older were minorities, with 38% Japanese, 14% Filipino, 8.7% Chinese, 7% Hawaiian, 2.1% Korean, and 2.8% other (EOA, 1998-a).

Figure 6: Ethnic Composition of Baby Boomers

In 1990 (In Percentage)

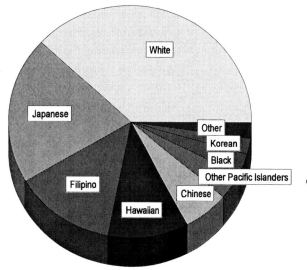

- In 1990, 20% of Hawai`i residents 60+ and 21% of residents 65+ (about one in five) were foreign born. In comparison, only 10% of the U.S. population 65+ was foreign-born in 1990. Among all the foreign-born, 10% were recent immigrants who arrived during the 1980s. (EOA 1997; U.S. BOC, 1992)

- In Hawai`i, 21% of the elderly population age 60+ had lived in Hawai`i less than 5 years. (EOA, 1997)

- The net migration of elderly 65+ in Hawai`i is almost 5.4%. (DBEDT, 1998-a)

- Nationwide, the proportion of Asian and Pacific Islander Americans in the country is estimated to double from 4.1% in 2000 to 8.7% by 2050.

- The U.S. Bureau of Census projects that minorities will represent 25% of citizens 65+ by 2030, up from 13% in 1990. If the number of permanent residents is added, the percentage will increase much more than 25%. (Davidhizar, 1996)

- In examining immigration patterns in Hawai`i, a majority of immigrants are from Asian countries. Filipinos are the largest group of immigrants, representing 55% of all immigrants since 1993 and 62% of all immigrants in 1996. Since Filipino birth rates are relatively high (20.6 per 1,000 in 1995), the number and proportion of Filipinos in the state will continue to grow. Since the birth rate of Japanese has been constantly low, the distribution of ethnic groups will be expected to alter greatly in the future. (Tables 13 and 14)

Education

Level of education often is associated with how well people manage their lives. Baby boomers
in Hawai'i have more years of education than boomers in the U.S. as a whole. Unlike the U.S. as
a whole, the educational attainment of Blacks in Hawai'i is quite high. Although currently
available data do not provide clear pictures of the educational attainment for each race in
Hawai'i, the majority of boomers are at least high school graduates.

- In 1990, about 25% (one in four) baby boomers in the U.S. had completed four or more
  years of college, compared with about 20% Americans ages 45-54. (Population Bulletin,
  1991) In 1998, 87.9% of baby boomers in the U.S. had completed high school or above
  and 27.5% had completed four years or more of college. (www.census.gov, 1996-b)

- Among Hawai'i baby boomers, 1990 statistics suggest that 90.9% had completed high
  school and 27.2% had earned at least a bachelors' degree. For the U.S. as a whole, only
  84.9% of boomers had completed high school and 24.9% had earned at least a bachelor's
  degree. (Figure 7, Table 15)

- In examining the trends of educational attainment between 1940 and 1990 in Hawai'i, the
  percentage of people who graduated from high school increased from 20.5% to 80.1%. In
  addition, the percentage of people who graduated from 4 years of college increased from
  5.3% to 22.9%. (Table 16)

- Overall, males had better educational attainment than females in Hawai'i, 81.7% vs.
  78.4% for high school completion and 24.4% vs. 21.4% for bachelor's degree or higher in
  1990. (Table 17)

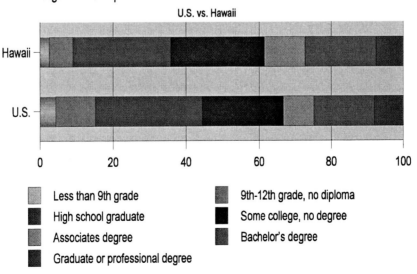

Figure 7: Comparison of Educational Attainment of Boomers in 1990
U.S. vs. Hawaii

- Overall, people in Honolulu County had better educational attainment than people in the other counties; 81.2% vs. 76.6% for high school completion and 24.6% vs. 17.8% for bachelor's degree or higher in 1990. (DBEDT,1997-a)

- Ethnically, 94.2% of Blacks in Hawai`i completed high school, followed by 89.3% of Whites, and 74.7% of Asian and Pacific Islanders in 1990. However, for Bachelor's degree or higher, Whites had the highest percent (30.2%) followed by Asian and Pacific Islanders (19.4%). (Figure 8, Table 18)

- In 1997, the ethnic distribution of people receiving degrees/certificates under the University of Hawai`i system was 22% Caucasian, 21% Japanese,13% Filipino, 10% Hawaiian/Part-Hawaiian, 10% Chinese, and 23% other. (Table 19)

- In 1990, about 5% of people 65 and older had difficulty speaking English in Hawai`i. Among minority groups, Koreans, Vietnamese, and Tongans had higher proportions of people who could not speak English at all or could not speak English very well. (Table 20)

- Among Hawai`i residents 60 and older, 26.6% were high school graduates and 7.4% were graduates of 4-year colleges in 1970. By 1980, these percentages increased to 40.1% and 10.7% of Hawai`i residents 60+ respectively. (EOA, 1996)

- With increasing availability of educational opportunities and more emphasis on life-long education, the educational level of the elderly population will rise when the baby boomers enter "old age."

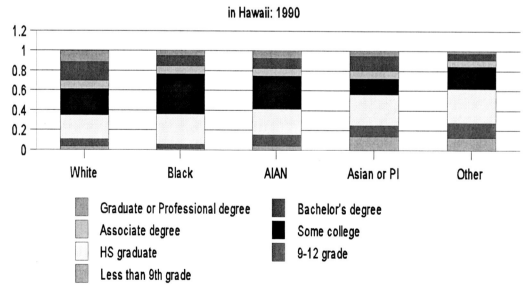

Figure 8: Educational Attainment of Baby Boomers in Hawaii: 1990

Marriage and Family

A little more than a half of Hawai`i baby boomers (62%) were married in 1990, compared to only one out of two (50%) baby boomers in the U.S. (www.census.gov). Hawai`i boomers have higher rates of divorce and remarriage compared to their U.S. counterparts and their parent's generation. Women in Hawai`i are, in general, getting married later and having fewer children than in previous generations, and men are marrying later than their female counterparts. For residents 65 and older, the percent of remarried couples has increased dramatically from 1960 to 1990 and the proportion of older women remarrying exceeded that of men.

- The number of children ever born to women in Hawai`i in 1960 was 2,250 per 1,000 women age 25-34 and 2,838 per 1,000 women age 35-44 (U.S. BOC, 1960). In 1980, it decreased to 1,333 per 1,000 women age 24-35 and 2,479 per 1,000 women age 35-44. (DBEDT,1987).

- In 1990, the number of children ever born to women in U.S. was 1,381 per 1,000 women age 26-34 and 1,960 per 1,000 women age 35-44 whereas in Hawai`i, it was 1,237 per 1,000 women age 26-34 and 1,812 per 1,000 women age 35-55. Therefore, the number of children born to women has been continuously decreasing. (www.census.gov, 1996-b)

- The average size of families in Hawai`i has been steadily decreasing from 4.29 in 1960 to 3.48 in 1990. (DBEDT, 1997-a)

- In Hawai`i in 1960, 82.2% of people age 25-44 were married (U.S. BOC, 1960). In comparison, only 62% of people age 25-44 were married (68% of leading-edge boomers and 54% of trailing-edge boomers) in 1990. (Table 21)

- In 1996, the marriage rate in Hawai`i was 15.8 per 1,000 population compared to 8.9 in the U.S. as a whole. The divorce rates, however, were slightly higher-- 4.6 per 1,000 in Hawai`i vs. 4.4 per 1,000 in the U.S. as a whole. (U.S. BOC, 1998)

- The overall marriage rate in Hawai`i decreased from 11.2 per 1,000 in 1950 to 9.4 per 1,000 in 1990. During the same time period, divorce rates increased from 2.4 per 1,000 to 4.7 per 1,000. (DBEDT, 1997-a)

- In Hawai`i, the median age of grooms increased from 29 years old in 1983 to 31 years old in 1990, while the median age of brides increased from 27 years old to 28 years old. (DBEDT, 1987 & 1991).

- In the U.S., the proportion of previously married adults in the 35-44 age group increased from 20.8% in 1980 to 31.3% in 1990 for males and from 25.6% in 1980 to 33.8% in 1990 for females. In Hawai`i, the percent of previously married adults increased from 36.6% in 1983 to 39.5% in 1990 for grooms and from 36.8% to 40.1% for brides. (Figure 9, Table 22).

- Among Hawai`i residents 60+, the proportions of currently married and never married were similar throughout the state. In Hawai`i County, 66.6% were married and 4.5% had never married. On O`ahu, 64.1% were married and 5.6% had never married. In Maui County, 66.4% were married and 4.5% had never married 4.5%. In Kaua`i County, 67.9% were married and 5.2% had never married. (EOA, 1998-b)

Figure 9 : Percent Previously Married Among Age 35-44 US vs. Hawaii: 1980-1990

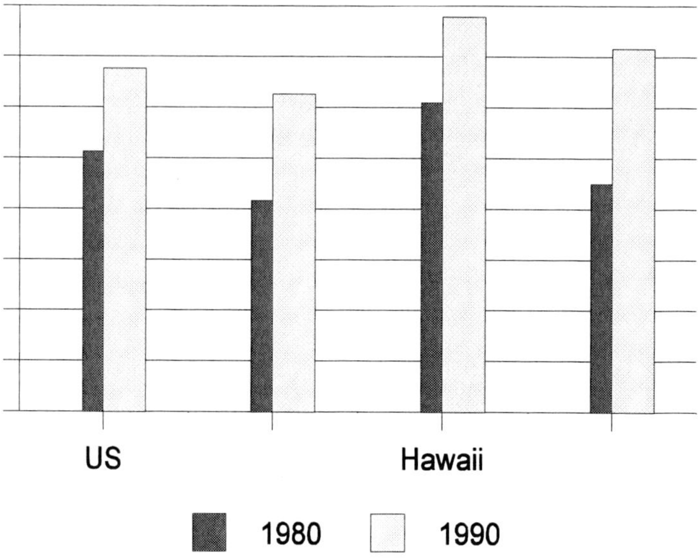

US   Hawaii

■ 1980   □ 1990

- Among Hawai`i residents 65+, 43% were married in 1990. (Table 23). Among this same group in 1995, only 2.7% reported having never married, compared to 5.2% of adults 65+ in the U.S. as a whole. (Table 23)

- The Social Security Administration projected that the proportion of married men 65 and older is expected to decline from 73 % in 1995 to 67% in 2050. The proportion of married women is expected to rise to 44% in 2030 and then decline to 42% in 2050. (www.aoa.dhhs.gov, 1996-b).

Household and Living Arrangements

Household size and composition are very important variables in describing current lifestyle and the living arrangements and to project future needs. Compared to the U.S. baby boomers as a whole, Hawai`i had fewer households headed by females, but had higher rates of non-family households and living with others. Only modest changes in the size and composition of family households are expected between 1990 and 2010.

- In Hawai`i, 45% of total households were headed by baby boomers in 1990. (EOA, 1996)

- In 1990, 89% of baby boomers in Hawai`i lived in urban areas, compared to only 76% of boomers in the U.S. as a whole. (www.census.gov, 1996-b)

- In 1990, 25.6% of Hawai`i boomers were living in non-family households (including those living alone and those living with unrelated others), compared to 23.7% of boomers in the U.S. as a whole. Only 10.3% of Hawai`i boomer households were headed by a female, compared to 13.5% of boomer households in the U.S. as a whole. (Table 24)

- Maui had the highest percentage of non-family households headed by baby boomers, 29% in 1990. Kaua`i had the lowest percentage of non-family households headed by baby boomers, 22% in 1990. (EOA, 1996)

- In 1990, more males lived alone than females in age groups under 60: 5.1% and 3.7% respectively. However, in the older age groups, more females lived alone than males: 19.4% and 10.6% respectively. A similar pattern is seen in all four counties. (Table 25)

- The U.S. Bureau of Census projects modest change in the distribution of family households from 70.5% in 1995 to 70.0% in 2010 and a slight decrease of a female householder from 11.4% to 10.9%. (www.census.gov, 1999-c)

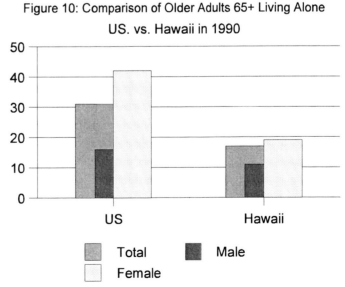

Figure 10: Comparison of Older Adults 65+ Living Alone US. vs. Hawaii in 1990

- According to the Bureau of Census, the percentage of persons 65+ living alone in the U.S. was 39.4% in 1998. About three times as many older women lived alone than older men. In Hawai`i, 16.8% of adults 65+ (23% of females and 11% of males) were living alone in 1990. (Figure 10, Table 25 & 26)

21

- In 1990, among adults 65+ with incomes at or below 125% of the official poverty level, 40% were living alone and 21% were living with unrelated others. Of females elders living alone, 41% were considered poor compared to only 32% of male elders living alone. Disparity among ethnic groups is also evident. Of Black elders living alone, 69% were considered poor compared to only 36% of White elders living alone. (www.aoa.dhhs.gov, 1996-b)

- By 2020, it is projected that 31% of Whites 65+ will live alone. For older Hispanics, the percent living alone is projected to increase from 22% in 1990 to 25% in 2020. For elders in other minority groups, the percent living alone is projected to increase from 30% in 1990 to 32% in 2020. (Table 26)

- It is projected that the elderly poor who live alone will decrease to 29% in 2005 and 20% in 2020. Among poor males, only 18% are expected to live alone in 2005 and this is expected to decrease to 10% in 2020. Among poor females, 32% are expected to live alone in 2005 and this is expected to decrease to 23% in 2020. For Whites, the proportion is expected to decrease to 25% in 2005 and 15% in 2020. While expected to decrease, the proportion of poor elderly Blacks and other minorities living alone will still be high, 53% in 2005 and 41% in 2020. (www.aoa.dhhs.gov, 1996-b)

Interstate Mobility

Baby boomers are said to be extremely mobile and available data suggest that baby boomers are more likely to move than previous generations. Movement, however, is more often intra-state rather than interstate in both the U.S. and Hawai`i.

- In1990, 56.2% of U.S. boomers and 56.3% of Hawai`i boomers changed their residences. Among boomers who changed the residence, 21% of U.S. boomers moved to a different state whereas 37.5% of Hawai`i boomers moved to a different state. (Figure 11, Table 27)

- More Hawai`i baby boomers lived abroad between 1985 and 1990 than their U.S. counterparts, 5.9% vs. 2.8%. However, the available data does not indicate the difference among immigrants and overseas returnees. (Table 27)

Figure 11: Interstate Mobility of Baby Boomers US vs. Hawaii: 1985 - 1990

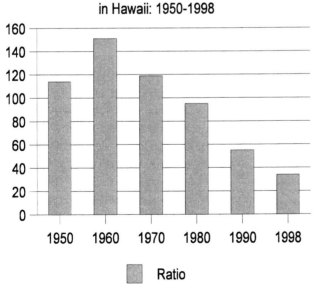

Figure 12: Ratio of Interstate Movement of Job Seeker in Hawaii: 1950-1998

- In examining the interstate movement of overall job seekers in Hawai`i, there was more net in-migration of workers to Hawai`i during the period 1950-1980 and more net out-migration of workers from Hawai`i since late 1980 to the present period. A particularly higher ratio of out-migration is noted since1990. (Figure 12, Table 28)

Financial Security of Baby Boomers

<u>Labor Force Participation and Economic Dependency</u>

The coming-of-age of the baby boomers has not only expanded the size of the labor force, it has changed its composition. More females are participating in the labor force than ever before and minorities are representing an increasing proportion of the labor force. The female participation of labor force in Hawai`i is much higher than in the U.S. as a whole. Labor-force participation rates in Hawai`i may not change much between 1995 to 2020.

- In 1990, 80% of Hawai`i female boomers were in the labor force, compared to only 75% of female baby boomers in the U.S. as a whole (Table29).

- In 1990, more Hawai`i female boomers with children were in the labor force than in the U.S. as a whole. For Hawai`i female boomers, 66.7% of those with children under age 6 and 83.3% of those with children age 6-17 were in the labor force. In comparison, only 39.7% female boomers with children under age 6 and 44.8% of female boomers with children 6-17 were in the labor force in the U.S. as a whole (<u>www.census.gov,</u> 1996-b).

- Female labor-force participation is higher in the boomer generation than in the preceding generation. In 1995, 77% of female boomers and 92% of male boomers were working, compared to only 55% of females and 95% of males in the cohort that preceded the baby boomers (Poulos, 1997).

- In 1960 in Hawai`i, 96.7% of men age 25-44 were in labor force, compared to 47.7% of women age 25-44 (U.S. BOC, 1960). In 1990, 80% of female baby boomers were in the labor force. (Figure 13, Table 30)

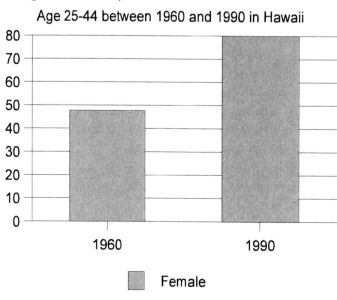

Figure 13: Comparison of Female Labor Force Age 25-44 between 1960 and 1990 in Hawaii

- The median age of workers in the U.S. was 38 in 1994 and will be 41 by 2005. The labor force will continue to age until about 2015. (Poulos, 1997)

- The U.S. labor force is projected to grow 1.3% yearly from 1990 to 2005 (Fullerton, 1991). In Hawai`i, the labor force participation rate is projected to remain stable over the next 20 years--67.6% in 1995, 67.1% in 2010, and 67.4% in 2020. (DBEDT, 1997-b)

- Comparing across ethnic groups, employment rates in 1997 were 89% for Hawaiians, 91% for African Americans, 93% for Caucasians and Filipinos, 94% for Koreans, 96% for Chinese, and 97% for Japanese. (Table 31)

- In 1990, the level of unemployment was 2.8% in Hawai`i; however, it is expected to increase to 5.1% in 2010 and slightly decrease to 4.7% in 2020. (Table 32)

- The island of Lanai had the lowest percentage of unemployment (3.5%) and the island of Molokai had the highest percentage of unemployment (15.0%) in 1998. Unemployment rates were 5.4% on O`ahu, 9.7% on the Big island, 9.8% on Kaua`i, and 6.6% on Maui. (DLIR, 1999)

- The retirement age of people in the U.S. has been getting younger, from age 68.7 in 1940 to 63.6 in 1995. Retirement at age 62 has recently become the norm in the U.S. (Table 33)

- In the U.S. as a whole, the dependency ratio (those 65+ per 100 working adults) is projected to increase from 20.9 in 1995 to 27.5 in 2020, an increase of 32%. However in Hawai`i, the dependency ratio will increase from 21.5% in 1995 to 30.0% in 2020, an increase of 40%. (Figure 14, Table 34)

- The parent support ratio (adults 85+ per 100 adults age 50 to 64) in the U.S. is expected to rise from 10.6 in 1995 to 10.9 in 2020, an increase of 3%. In Hawai`i, it is projected to increase by 80%, 15.7 per 100 by 2020. (Figure 14, Table 34)

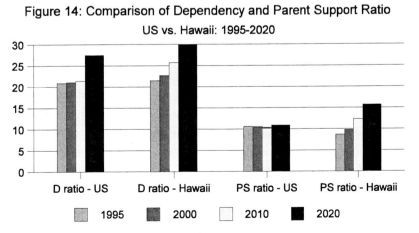

Figure 14: Comparison of Dependency and Parent Support Ratio
US vs. Hawaii: 1995-2020

Income and Poverty

The median income of the baby boomers in Hawai`i is higher than that of U.S. baby boomers as a whole. Likewise, the income of older adults in Hawai`i is higher than that of their U.S. counterparts. However, Hawai`i's cost of living is much higher. The percentage of residents below the poverty level is lower than in the U.S. as a whole. Similarly, however, households headed by females and ethnic minorities were less advantaged than the households headed by males.

- In the U.S. in1989, median household income was $34,601 and median family income was $36,434 for baby boomers. In Hawai`i in 1989, median household income was $38,367 while median family income was $40,079 for the boomer group. Compared to the U.S. baby boomers, Hawai`i baby boomers had higher household and family median incomes. (Table 35)

- In general, Honolulu County had the highest overall median income, $40,581, for all households in 1989. Hawai`i county had the lowest median income, $29,712, in 1989. (DBEDT, 1997-a)

- In Hawai`i in1989, 6.9% of boomers were living below the poverty level compared to 10% of baby boomers in the U.S. as a whole.

- The percentage of adults living below the poverty level increases with age. For example, 11.3% of adults 65 and older lived in poverty, while 16.7% of adults 75 and older lived in poverty in 1990. (Table 36)

- In the U.S. in 1990, 11.5% of all families and 37.2% of households headed by female baby boomers were below poverty. In Hawai`i, 7.8% of all families and 30.4% of households headed by female baby boomers were below poverty. (www.census.gov, 1996-b)

- In 1996 in Hawai`i, South Pacific Islanders such as Samoans and Tongans, had the largest percentage of people whose income was below $10,000 (35.3%) and Japanese had the largest percentage of people whose income was above $75,000 (15.6%). (DOH, 1996)

- In the U.S. in 1996, 36.7% of Black elders (65+) and 36.2% of Hispanic elders (65+) were living in poverty or near poverty, compared to only 16.7% of White elders and 14.3% of Asian and Pacific Islanders elders. (Table 37)

- In Hawai`i, about 11% of minority elders and 12% of White elders were considered to be low-income. (Table 38)

Social Security and Pensions

Social Security and pensions are the two major sources of income for retirees. Social Security is projected to become exhausted in 2030 when all the baby boomers are 65 and older. Moreover, the revenues will be sufficient to pay only about 75% of benefits due. In Hawai`i, 80% of adults 65 and older received Social Security income. Overall, the proportion of people vested in pension plans has increased since the 970s.

- In Hawai`i, 80% of adults 65 and older received Social Security income and 23% had some income from earnings (jobs) in 1989. Only 39% received income from pensions (retirement income). (Table 39)

- The total number of beneficiaries of Social Security in Hawai`i was 169,000 in 1996. Of these beneficiaries, 78% were retired workers and their dependents, 13% were survivors, and 8.9% were disabled workers and their dependents. (U.S. BOC, 1998-b)

- In 1996, the average monthly Social Security benefit in Hawai`i was $733 for retired workers, $717 for disabled workers, and $676 for widows and widowers. (U.S. BOC, 1998-b)

- Social Security was the major source of income among elders with the lowest quartile of income, whereas earnings was the major source of income for elders in the highest quartile of income. (Table 40)

- In 1998, 52% of the employers of baby boomers offered pension plans and 44.4% of baby boomer employees were participating in pension plan provided by the employer. (www.census.gov, Ferret, 1999-b)

<u>Assets and Savings</u>

Although there are contradictory views about the saving habits of baby boomers, many data sources present rather gloomy data. As far as assets are concerned, Hawai`i baby boomers have lower rates of home ownership than U.S. baby boomers.

- More than half (57%) of U.S. baby boomers owned their own homes in 1990. Among them, more leading-edge boomers owned a home (66%) than trailing-edge boomers (44%). In Hawai`i, only 41% of baby boomers owned their own homes. (Figure 15, Table 42)

- Among Hawai`i baby boomers in 1997, only 53.8% in Honolulu County owned a home, compared to 65.0% in Maui County, 67.2% in Hawai`i County, and 67.1% in Kaua`i County. (DBEDT 1997-a)

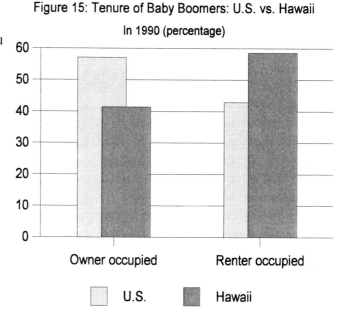

Figure 15: Tenure of Baby Boomers: U.S. vs. Hawaii In 1990 (percentage)

- In Hawai`i, 72.1% of adults 60 and older were home-owners in 1990, but the percentage of elders with homes decreases with age. About 74% of adults age 65 to 74 owned homes, while only 62.9% of adults 85 and older owned homes. (Figure 16, Table 43)

- Similar to baby boomers' home ownership patterns, Honolulu county had the lowest percentage of home ownership among older adults age 60+ (70%) compared to 78% of elders in Hawai`i County, 78% of elders in Maui County and 76% of elders in Kaua`i County. (Table 44)

- The average monthly mortgage was highest in Honolulu. It has increased tremendously over the years, from $821 in 1992 to $1,430 in 1997. (Table 45)

- Consumer saving years have generally been associated with the ages 45 to 60. In 1995, however, personal (household) savings, as a percent of personal disposable income, was 4.5% in the United States in 1995. Compared to 1980, the percent of saving has been reduced by about one-half (Vincenzino, 1996).

- According to Merrill Lynch, the retirement saving adequacy of baby boomers (all households) in 1996 was 35.9%. This report suggested that baby boomers need to save three times more for retirement than they're now saving (Bernheim,1997).

- A survey conducted by the American Association of Retired Persons indicated that a typical boomer has accumulated about $40,000 in total net worth as of 1994 (in current dollars), not including Social Security and pension wealth. Excluding home equity, leading and trailing-edge boomers assets totaled nearly $18,000 and $7,000, respectively (www.aarp.org, 1999)

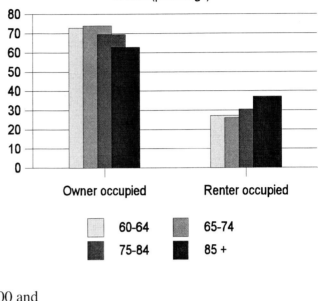

Figure 16: Tenure of Older Adults in Hawaii
In 1990 (percentage)

- Another retirement study conducted by AARP (1999) categorized boomers in five distinct groups (www.aarp.org, 1999):

  o The Strugglers: The 9% of boomers who are low income and not saving any money for retirement.
  o The Anxious: The 23% of boomers with household incomes about $10,000 below that of the average boomer, who are striving to save but unlikely will be able to save enough.
  o The Traditionalists: The 25% of boomers who plan both to work and to rely on Social Security and Medicare in retirement.
  o The Enthusiasts: The 13% of boomers who are eager to retire and do not plan to work at all during retirement, able to rely on savings, family, and Social Security.
  o The Self Reliants: The 30% of boomers at the highest income and educational levels who are aggressively investing money for a comfortable retirement.

Health Status and Long-Term Care

Health Behaviors

Overall, Hawai`i baby boomers have healthier lifestyles than their U.S. counterparts, except in the area of alcohol consumption. Within Hawai`i, however, baby boomers have relatively poor lifestyle behaviors and appear to be leading unhealthier lives now than in 1990, as the prevalence of drinking and overweight has increased substantially. More Hawai`i elders get flu and pneumonia vaccinations compared to their U.S. counterparts. If these trends continue, and baby boomers can get control over their drinking and their weight, baby boomers may be more successful than past generations at delaying disability and death.

- In 1997, people in Hawai`i had healthier life styles, i.e., less smoking, fewer people overweight, and more people using seat belts, compared to people on the mainland. However, for both acute and chronic drinking, Hawai`i rated higher than the U.S., 17% vs. 15% and 5% vs. 3% respectively (Table 46)

- In 1990, Hawai`i boomers had healthier life styles than their U.S. counterparts in all areas expect drinking. For both the U.S. and Hawai`i, leading edge baby boomers had healthier life styles than trailing edge boomers. However, leading edge boomers in U.S. had more weight problems than trailing edge boomers. On the contrary, trailing edge boomers in Hawai`i had more weight problems than leading edge boomers. (Figure 17, Table 47)

- The prevalence of acute drinking among baby boomers in Hawai`i increased from 14% in 1990 to 19% in 1998. Also, the prevalence of smoking increased slightly from 20% in 1990 to 21% in 1998. (Table 47 & 48)

- In 1998, leading edge boomers in Hawai`i had unhealthier lifestyles than trailing edge boomers except for acute drinking. (Figure 18, Table 48)

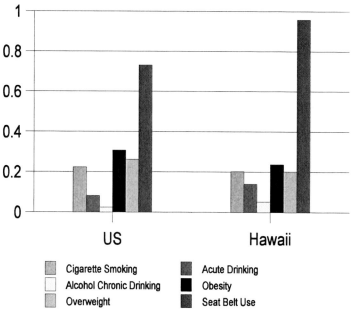

Figure 17 : Comparison of Health Risk Factors among Boomers: US vs. Hawaii

Legend:
- Cigarette Smoking
- Alcohol Chronic Drinking
- Overweight
- Acute Drinking
- Obesity
- Seat Belt Use

- In 1995, 9.2% of adults 65+ smoked cigarettes in Hawai`i, much less than the younger generation (26.2% for age 25-54) and much less than their U.S. counterparts (14.3% of U.S. male elders and 11.5% of U.S. female elders). (www2.cdc.gov, 1999; U.S. BOC, 1998)

- A majority of baby boomers in Hawai`i (80.4%) reported being physically active or somewhat active in 1998, though 74.2% of them did not have regular and sustained leisure time physical activity in 1998. Only 1.3% of boomers reported poor health status in the same year. (Table 48)

- People in Maui County had the highest percentage of obesity (30.1%) but Honolulu County had the highest percentage of people with a sedentary lifestyle (48.4%) and without regular physical activity/exercise (72.4%) in 1996. (www.Hawaii.gov,1997)

- Overall, Hawaiians had the highest proportion of health risk factors (e.g., smoking, alcohol drinking, and overweight) among Hawai`i's major ethnic groups. (www.Hawaii.gov,1999)

- Very few of Hawai`i baby boomers got vaccinations for flu or pneumonia in 1997; only 22.1% and 5.9% respectively. However, 71.1% of adults 65 and above got flu shots in 1997, an increase over 62.3% in 1995. In addition, 51.7% of older adults got vaccinated for pneumonia in 1997, compared to only 43.0% in 1995. (DOH, 1999)

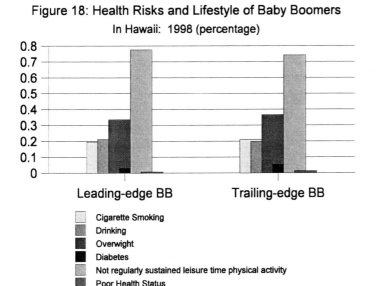

Figure 18: Health Risks and Lifestyle of Baby Boomers In Hawaii: 1998 (percentage)

Leading-edge BB   Trailing-edge BB

- Cigarette Smoking
- Drinking
- Overwight
- Diabetes
- Not regularly sustained leisure time physical activity
- Poor Health Status

- Compared to the U.S., Hawai`i's older adults have better preventive habits such as non-smoking and exercise than their U.S. counterparts. In 1997, only 65.9% of U.S. elders got a flu vaccination and 45.8% got a pneumonia vaccination. (Table 49)

Prevalence of Major Diseases

The prevalence of major diseases and chronic conditions increases with age. As baby boomers enter "old age," they will become more susceptible to diseases and disability. In Hawai`i, men tend to be at higher risk of having heart problems than women. On the other hand, women tend to be at higher risk of having cancer and diabetes than men. Comparing ethnic groups, Caucasians have the higher prevalence rates of malignant neoplasm and Japanese and Chinese have a higher prevalence of diabetes, heart conditions and hypertension. The highest prevalence of asthma was noted among Hawaiians.

- The incidence of cancer (all cases) in Hawai`i was lower for both males and females than in the U.S. as a whole between 1990 and 1994.  For males, it was 425.7 per 100,000 in Hawai`i, compared to 485.1 per 100,000 nationwide. For females, it was 309.8 per 100,000 in Hawai`i, compared to 342.4 per 100,000 nationwide.  (HMSA,1999)  However, the Department of Health projects that the prevalence rates of malignant neoplasms in the future will continue to increase in Hawai`i. (Table50)

- The most prevalent chronic conditions for Hawai`i residents 65 and older are arthritis, high blood pressure, heart disease, and hearing impairment. The incidence of most chronic conditions increases with age, especially arthritis, diabetes, and hypertension. (Table 51)

- In 1998, Hawaiians had the highest rates of asthma, Japanese had the highest rates of hypertension and diabetes, and Chinese had the highest rates of arthritis. (Table 52)

- The baby boomers have higher rates of emotional disorders (depression, suicide, anxiety, alcohol and drug abuse) than previous generations. (Koenig, 1994)

- In the U.S. as a whole, the number of elders (65+) with diabetes is expected to increase from 3.3 million in 1990 to 4.1 million in 2010 and to 6.8 million in 2030. The prevalence of diabetes in adults 65+ is more than double that of adults 45-64 years old, 103.9 per 1,000 population vs. 51.8 per 1,000 population. (Helms, 1992)

- The incidence of Alzheimer's disease is approximately 50% in people over 80 years of age compared to10% among adults 65 years and older. (Chernoff, 1995)

- In the U.S., it is projected that almost 160 million people will have chronic conditions by 2040, an increase of 50% from 1995. (The Robert Wood Johnson Foundation, 1996)

Leading Causes of Death

The leading causes of death are quite similar among younger and older adults, except for suicide and accidents. Heart disease and malignant neoplasm are the two leading causes of death in the U.S., as well as in Hawai`i. Unless some major advances in medical technology occur in the near future, the current trends will continue when baby boomers enter "old age."

- Overall, Hawai`i had lower mortality rates for leading causes of death than did the U.S. as a whole in 1995. For example, the death rate for heart disease in Hawai`i was 196.0 per 100,000, compared to 280.7 per 100,000 for the U.S. as a whole. (Figure 19, Table 53)

- In 1995 in Hawai`i, the leading causes of death among baby boomers were malignant neoplasm (157 cases), heart diseases (122 cases), and accidents (101 cases). Suicide among baby boomers was also high (69 cases) compared to other causes of death. (DOH, 1995)

- Among people age 25-44, deaths from cancer, motor vehicle accidents, and suicide increased from 1950 to 1996. However, deaths from heart disease decreased from 16.4% in 1950 to 15.0% in 1996. (Table 54)

Figure 19: Selected Death Rates by Leading Causes for All Ages between U.S. and Hawaii: 1995

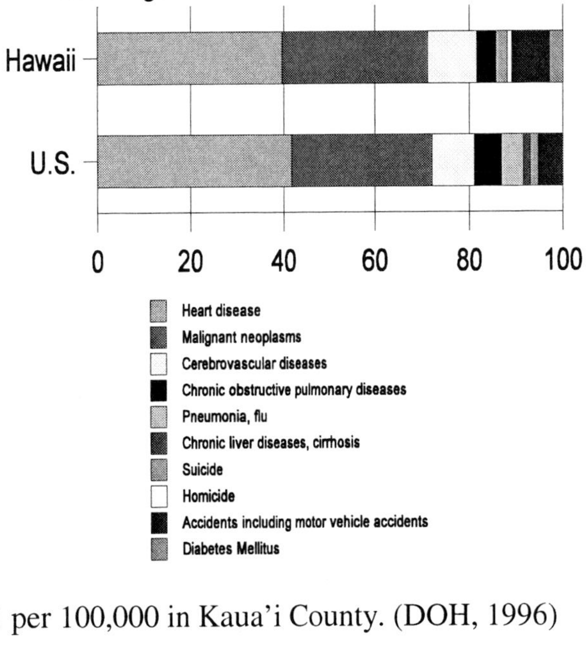

Heart disease
Malignant neoplasms
Cerebrovascular diseases
Chronic obstructive pulmonary diseases
Pneumonia, flu
Chronic liver diseases, cirrhosis
Suicide
Homicide
Accidents including motor vehicle accidents
Diabetes Mellitus

- In 1997, malignant neoplasm, heart disease, accidents (both unintentional injury and motor vehicle), and suicide were the leading causes of deaths among adults age 25 to 64 in Hawai`i. The major causes of deaths among adults age 65+ were heart disease, malignant neoplasm, cerebrovascular disease, influenza/pneumonia, and diabetes mellitus. (Table 55)

- Hawai`i County had the highest total death rate in 1996, 768.7 per 100,000, compared to 637.4 per 100,000 in Honolulu Country, 665.2 per 100,000 in Maui County, and 714.1 per 100,000 in Kaua'i County. (DOH, 1996)

- Among adults 65 and older, the percent of death from cerebrovascular disease, diabetes mellitus, heart disease, and suicide have decreased from 1950 to 1996. However, death from cancer and influenza/pneumonia have increased. (Table 56)

<u>Disability Rates and Nursing Home Population</u>

Limitation of usual activities is one of the measures of health status. In general, the number of adults with disabilities will increase as the number of older adults in the population increases. When the baby boomers enter "old age," the number of disabled adults will most likely increase dramatically. However, the percent of older adults in nursing homes may not necessarily increase in the near future if we expand home and community based care options.

- In 1990, 6.1% of U.S. baby boomers had a work disability and 3.7% had limitations in mobility or self-care. Whereas in Hawai`i, disability levels were 5.0% and 3.0% respectively. (www.census.gov, 1996-b)

- In Hawai`i, it is projected that the absolute and relative numbers of disabled older adults will increase from 25.8% (28,231 persons) between 1991-1995 to 30.9% (55,027 persons) between 2016-2020. (EOA, 1991)

- In the United States, it is projected that the number of adults 65+ with activity limitations will increase from 11.8 million in 1994 to16 million in 2010 and to 27.5 million in 2030, when all baby boomers are 65 or older. (Table 57)

- In the U.S., the number of disabled elders residing in the community is expected to increase from 9.2 million in 1990 to19-22 million in 2030, when all baby boomers are 65 or older. (Table 58)

- The National Long-Term Care Survey (NLTCS) indicated an accelerating decline in disability rates among the adults 65 and older between 1982 and 1994, and projected that a continued decline of 1.5% per annum is achievable. However, the increasing numbers of older adults will push upwards despite a small decline in the proportion of seniors who have disabilities.

- In the U.S., the number of nursing home residents 65 and older is projected to increase from 1.3 million in 1994 to 2 million in 2010 and to 3.3 million in 2030. (Rice, 1996)

- In examining the average occupancy of long-term care facilities in Hawai`i, the occupancy rate has been decreasing from 93.4% in 1991 to 90.5% in 1998. (Table 59)

- In Hawai`i, it is projected that the number of older adults requiring some type of formal paid home care will grow about 7% each year; i.e., more than 12,000 persons by 2020. (EOA, 1991)

Health and Long-Term Care Insurance

Medical costs and long-term care costs have increased tremendously over the last several decades. Consequently, insurance costs have increased as well. Though the percentage of uninsured Hawai`i residents was less than the U.S. as a whole in 1995, the uninsured population has been increasing in Hawai`i. Rates of insurance vary by ethnic group, with Caucasians having the highest percentage of uninsured people and Japanese having the lowest percentage of uninsured people. More leading-edge boomers seem to be without health insurance than trailing-edge boomers in Hawai`i. Although no figures were available regarding the people who are covered by private long-term care insurance in Hawai`i, in general, the number has been increasing and will likely continue to increase in the near future.

- In 1995, 5.7% of Hawai`i residents were uninsured, compared to 8.9% nationwide. The uninsured population increased to 6.0% in 1998, but it is still much lower than in the U.S. as a whole (16.3%). (Table 60)

- In 1998, 5.7% of leading-edge boomers in Hawai`i were uninsured, compared to 4.4% of trailing-edge boomers. (DOH, 1999)

- Honolulu County had the lowest percentage of uninsured people age 35-54 of the state's four counties in 1998. Relatively more trailing-edge boomers were uninsured in Honolulu and Hawai`i Counties, but the opposite was true for Maui and Kaua`i Counties. (Table 61)

- In 1998, 9% of Caucasian in Hawai`i were uninsured, compared to only 3% of Japanese. (Table 61)

- Among insured baby boomers in Hawai`i, the most common type of coverage was through employment organizations--63.5% for leading-edge boomers and 61.3% for trailing-edge boomers. (Table 62)

- The number of private insurance agencies providing long-term care insurance in the U.S. has increased from 30 in 1986 to 125 in 1995. Currently, about 4.35 million people have long-term care policies. However, private long-term care insurance financed less than 1% of long-term care services received in 1995 ($700 million out of $90.9 billion) (Cunningham, 1998; U.S. House of Representatives,1998)

- Currently, the proportion of elderly who can afford long-term care insurance ranges from 10%-20%. (US House of Representatives, 1998) In Hawai`i, less than 8% of the general population and 12% of adults 65+ are expected to have private long-term care insurance. (EOA, 1991)

- In Hawai`i, long-term care insurance will likely pay less than 6 tenths of one percent (0.6%) of all nursing home costs by 2020. (EOA, 1991)

Medicare Expenditures

Health care expenditures have been increasing rapidly over the last several decades and are expected to continue rising as the baby boomers enter "old age." National health care expenditures are projected to increase to $16 trillion in 2030, when all baby boomers are Medicare eligible, and 25.9% of national health care expenditures will be paid for by the Medicare program. As expenditures increase, and the burden on government and retirement payment systems grows, baby boomers may be forced to consider alternative ways to cover their health care costs when they retire, rather than depending solely on Medicare.

- In 1993, personal health care expenditures in Hawai`i totaled $3.5 billion, spent primarily for hospital care (41.9%) and physician services (22.1%). (HMSA, 1999)

- In the U.S., personal health care expenditures for adults 65 and older are projected to increase from $31 billion in 1994 to $384 billion in 2010 and to $665 billion in 2030. (Rice, 1996)

- 3.9% ($30.9 billion) of the total national personal health care expenditures was spent for home health care services. Home health care expenditures are projected to increase to $68 billion by 2005. (Rice, 1996)

- National health expenditures are projected to rise from $666 billion in 1990 to $1.7 trillion in 2000, an amount equal to 18% of the U.S. gross domestic product (GDP), and to $16 trillion in 2030, or 32% of the GDP. (Figure 20, Tables 63 and 64)

- In 1995, the total number of enrollees for Medicare in Hawai`i was 149,000 and the payments made on their behalf totaled $580 million. (U.S. BOC, 1998-b)

Figure 20: Projection of National Health Expenditure in U.S.: 1990 - 2030

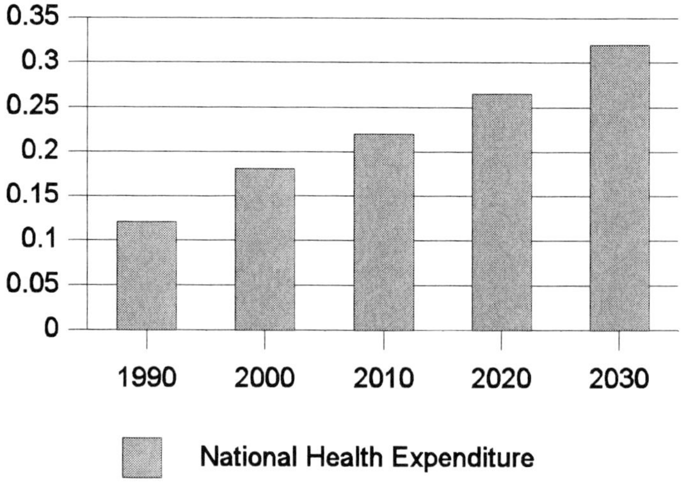

National Health Expenditure

- Medicare's share of the National Health Expenditure is expected to rise to 18.8% in 2000 and to 25.9% by 2030, when all baby boomers are Medicare-eligible. (Table 66)

- In the U.S., Medicare hospital insurance (HI) spending for inpatient services and Medicare supplementary medical insurance (SMI) spending for outpatient services in 1990 accounted for 26.7% of hospital patient revenue. Medicare HI and SMI spending is projected to account for 34.9% of hospital patient revenue in 2030. (Table 66)

36

- Medicare hospital insurance is financed through a payroll tax on wages and self-employment earnings. In 1990, Medicare hospital insurance spending was 2.7% of taxable payroll. It is projected to rise to 3.8% in 2000 and to 8.6% in 2030. (Table 66)

- In 2010, the trust fund for Medicare Part A (covering hospitalizations) will become insolvent. (U.S. Senate, 1998)

Medicaid and Expenditures for Long-Term Care

Medicaid and long-term care expenditures have been increasing rapidly over the last several decades and are expected to continue rising as the baby boomers enter "old age." About 13% of the $832 billion of personal health care expenditures in 1994 were spent on long-term care, almost 40% of which was paid by Medicaid. The majority (70%) of long-term care expenditures for elders is for nursing homes, which cost about $40,000 per patient per year in 2000, but are expected to cost $204,000 a year by 2020. As expenditures increase, baby boomers may be forced to consider alternative ways to cover long-term care, rather than relying solely on Medicaid.

- About 13% of the $832 billion in personal health care expenditures in 1994 was spent on long-term care. Of this total, 38% was paid by Medicaid, 20% by Medicare or other public sources, 42% from private sources. Less than 5% was paid by long-term care insurance. (Rice, 1996)

- According to the 1991 National Health Provider Inventory, about 4.2% of the adults 65 and older were in nursing homes. The major sources of payment for nursing home care were Medicaid and out-of-pocket payments.

- For community-based long-term care, Medicare was the major source of payment and private insurance covered only 1% of the expenditures. (Table 65)

- Nursing home care expenditures in Hawai`i represented 5.2% of total personal health care expenditures in 1993. Nationally, nursing home expenditures represented 8.5% of total personal health care expenditure in 1997, but are expected to increase to 10% by 2030. (DBEDT, 1997-a; Burner, 1992)

- In 1995, the cost of long-term nursing home care was more than $40,000 per patient per year, and 70% of total elderly long-term care expenditures were for nursing homes. (Scanlon, 98; U.S. House of Representative, 1998) In Hawai`i, the cost for nursing home care was similar to the U.S., but it is projected to increase to $204,000 per patient per year by 2020. (EOA, 1991)

- By 2020 in Hawai`i, long-term care costs including nursing home and home care services will increase to more than 1,100% of the 1991 value from $181 million to $2050 million. (EOA, 1991)

- In 1994, 12% of the 35.1 million Medicaid recipients in the U.S. were 65 years or older, accounting for 31% of total Medicaid expenditures. (Rice, 1996)

- In 1995, the total number of Medicaid recipients in Hawai`i was 52,000, for whom payments totaling $258 million were made. (U.S. BOC, 1998) The number of elderly who are Medicaid qualified at entry into nursing home will increase from 1,500 for the period 1991-95 to 3,250 for the period 2016-20. However, the relative proportion of Medicaid to non-Medicaid admissions remains fairly constant at about 48% (EOA, 1991)

- In Hawai`i, the state share of Medicaid expenditures will increase from 40.2 million to 558.7 million from 1991 to 2020. (EOA, 1991)

- Between 1991 and 2020, the Hawai`i state portion of expenditures for the Medicaid program for elderly nursing home care will increase by almost 1,300% to $495 million. (EOA, 1991)

- Most (77%) of Medicaid expenditures for long-term care services in Hawai`i has been spent for ICF care, 23% for SNF care, and 0.4% for Hospice care in 1998, totaling about $137 million. The expenditure for hospice service has increased from 0.1% in 1993 to 0.4% in 1998. (Loke, 2000).

Informal Support for Long-Term Care

A shortage of informal caregiving (support provided by family, relatives, and friends without any monetary compensation) is predicted when baby boomers enter "old age." Some of the reasons for this include: baby boomers have fewer children than past generations; they have higher rates of marital dissolution; an increased number of older adults are living alone; more women have joined the labor force; and attitudes toward filial responsibility have changed. The circumstances of the adult children affect their parents' living arrangements; nevertheless, it seems that reciprocity, not dependency, dominates the relationship between adult children and their parents until the very late years (Silverstone, 1996).

- Adult daughters provide almost one-third of long-term care in the United States. (Marosy, 1997)

- In Hawai`i, family members provided care to fully half of all disabled elderly in 1991. The number of disabled elderly cared for by family members is expected to increase from about 10,000 in 1990 to 25,000 by 2020. (EOA, 1991)

- According to a survey conducted for Hawai`i Government employees in 1990, approximately 24% of all state employee households provide assistance to older adults age 60+. Among them, 68% of caregivers were female. A majority of caregivers were baby boomers and their median income was $50,745. (Table 67)

- The types of services provided by informal caregivers included assistance with activities of daily living (ADLs, such as bathing, dressing, and eating) and with instrumental activities of daily living (IADLs, such as cooking, cleaning, providing transportation, and taking care of finances). (EOA, 1990)

- Hawai`i government employees who were caregivers were spending an average of 8-9 hours per week assisting their care recipients with their ADLs and IADLs in 1990. (EOA, 1990)

- It is expected that there will be a shortage of informal caregivers when baby boomers themselves enter "old age." There is uncertainty regarding the patterns of caregiving by informal caregivers since the relationship between parents and children are changing. Some of the factors influencing the changing relationships are separation and divorce, fewer children born to baby boomers, and lower rates of marriage among baby boomers.

Formal Support for Long-Term Care

Although various formal long-term care support services are currently available in Hawai`i, a shortage of formal support services is expected when the baby boomers enter "old age." It is imperative to examine the availability of human resources, such as nurses, social workers, and particularly para-professional workers, to provide a continuum of care and to support independent living of elders.

- The number of long-term care facilities has increased from 33 in 1980 (a total bed capacity of 2,656) to 45 in 1998 (a total bed capacity of 3,991) and another 598 beds are under construction. The number of adult residential care facilities also increased from 283 (a total bed capacity of 1,573) in 1980 to 508 (a total bed capacity of 2,609) in 1997. (DOH, 1999, Table 68)

- In 1998, Hawai`i's formal support services included 45 long-term care facilities (approved by State Health Planning & Development Agency), 508 adult residential care facilities, 6 adult day health/day hospitals, and 16 adult day care centers. (Table 68)

- The number of home health agencies in the United States has increased from 6,000 participating facilities in 1986 to 10,807 in 1998, an increase of 80.1% (www.hcfa.gov, 1998)

- Although there is some information about health care providers in Hawai`i, there is no comprehensive information regarding human resources in the social service sector, such as social workers and para-professionals. (Table 69)

- It seems that Home Health Aides and Personal/Home Care Aides are fast growing occupations in Hawai`i. The percent increase from 1996 to 2006 is expected to be 75.0% (560 to 980) and 74.4% (1,330 to 2,320), respectively. (www.state.hi.us, 1999)

- It is projected that the number of elderly using formal paid community services will double between 1991 and 2020, from 9500 to 20,700 users annually, an increase of over 1000% (or about 8% annually). (EOA, 1991)

- Hawai`i's long-term care facilities utilize slightly fewer nursing personnel per bed than the U.S. as a whole, with a combined total of 0.64 staff per bed compared with the U.S. total of 0.66 per bed. (Table 70).

PART IV
DISCUSSION

Review of Major Findings

Hawai`i's elderly population is growing, and is growing much faster than the nation as a whole. By 2011, the first boomers will reach the conventional retirement age of 65 and by 2030, all baby boomers will be 65 or older. This means that:

- Residents 60 and older comprised 16% of our population in 1990. By 2020, the number of residents 60+ will have doubled over 1990, to represent 25% of the population.

- Residents 65 and older (those eligible for Social Security and Medicare) will more than double; they comprised 11% of the total population in 1990 but will account for 18% in 2020. If military personnel and their dependents are excluded from the projections, the population 65+ will account for 20% in 2020.

- Residents 85 and older (those most in need of institutional, community, and in-home services due to high levels of disability, both mental and physical) comprised 1% of our total population in 1990. By 2020, the number of residents 85+ will have more than tripled, to represent 2.6% of the total population.

What is a typical baby boomer in Hawai`i? Existing data from a number of federal and state sources suggest:

Profile of a Typical Hawai`i Baby Boomer		
The typical boomer in Hawai`i is an Asian or Pacific Islander and a high school graduate (only 27% are college graduates). He/she most likely lives in a family household, having married at around age 30. He/she has a job and his/her family income is about $40,000. The typical boomer wears seatbelts, does not smoke or drink, and is not overweight. If this boomer were to die, he/she would be likely to die from cancer, heart disease, or injury. But the majority of boomers can expect to live another 25 to 45 years. He/she does not own a home (only 41% do). His/her parents are still living, and the boomer may expect to inherit property or income from them. No Hawai`i data are available, but national data suggest our typical boomer is not saving regularly for retirement (only 42% are) and is not participating in a pension plan (only 44% are).	Asian/Pacific Islander	57%
	High school grad	91%
	College grad	27%
	Mean age of groom	31 years
	Mean age of bride	28 years
	Lives in non-family household	26%
	Female in labor force	80%
	Median family income	$40,079
	Cigarette smoking	20%
	Acute (binge) drinking	14%
	Chronic drinking	5%
	Overweight	24%
	Obesity	31%
	Seatbelt user	96%
	Owns a home	41%
	National data:	
	Saving for retirement	42%
	Participating in pension plan	44%

How do Hawai`i's baby boomers compare to the previous generation (i.e., Hawai`i's current seniors citizens)? How do they compare with U.S. baby boomers as a whole? Existing data from a number of federal and state sources suggest:

In Comparison to Today's Senior Citizens/Parents Generation Hawaii Baby Boomers:	In Comparison to U.S. Boomers as a Whole Hawaii Baby Boomers:
<ul><li>will live longer than today's senior citizens.</li><li>have more formal education than today's senior citizens.</li><li>have higher median family and household incomes than today's senior citizens, but the cost of living is much higher today than it was 20-40 years ago.</li><li>will have more females participating in the labor force than their parent's generation.</li><li>have fewer children than their parent's generation.</li><li>have higher rates of divorce and remarriage than their parent's generation.</li><li>are less likely to own a home than their parent's generation.</li><li>are much more likely to smoke, drink, and be overweight.</li></ul>	<ul><li>will live longer than mainland boomers.</li><li>have more formal education than mainland boomers.</li><li>have higher median family income, but the cost of living in Hawai`i is higher than on the mainland.</li><li>have more females in the labor force, compared to mainland boomers.</li><li>have fewer children than boomers in the U.S. as a whole.</li><li>have higher rates of divorce and remarriage than mainland boomers.</li><li>are less likely to own their own homes.</li><li>are less likely to smoke, more likely to drink, and more likely to use seatbelts,compared to baby boomers on the mainland,.</li></ul>

Other facts about baby boomers include:

- Baby boomers are more diverse than their parent's generation and will expect more role options as seniors.

- Baby boomers are more consumer-oriented than their parent's generation, and more likely to challenge authority and demand attention and services.

- Many boomers are not saving for retirement. A survey by the American Association for Retired People (AARP) found that only 42% reported saving regularly for retirement and did not have a large store of assets. Excluding house equity, leading-edge boomers (those born 1946-1955) had only $18,000 in assets while trailing-edge boomers (those born 1956-1964) had only $7,000 in assets.

- According to Merrill Lynch, the retirement saving adequacy of baby boomers (all households) in 1996 was 35.9%. This report suggested that baby boomers need to save three times more for retirement than they're now saving (Bernheim, 1997).

- Hawai`i's dependency ratio (the ratio of adults 65+ to working-age adults) will increase, from 21.5 older adults per 100 working-age adults in 1995 to 30 older adults to 100 working-age adults in 2020. This represents an increase of 40%, compared to an increase of only 32% for the U.S. as a whole. Thus, Hawai`i will have a shrinking number of working-age adults (who contribute to the tax base) trying to support a growing number of adults 65+ (who use many of the services supported by state and federal taxes).

- Hawai`i's parent's support ratio (the ratio of adults 85+ per adults 50-64, who are most likely to be family caregivers) will increase from 8.7 adults 85+ per 100 family caregivers in 1995 to 15.7 adults 85+ per 100 family caregivers in 2020.

- U.S. health care costs for adults 65+ are projected to increase from $31 billion in 1994 to $665 billion in 2030, an increase of over 2000%. Many aging boomers may expect Medicare to cover these costs.

- In Hawai`i, long-term care costs, including nursing homes and home care services, will increase from 181 million in 1990 to 2,050 million in 2020, an increase of over 1,000%. It is projected that less than 10% of Hawai`i's population will have a private long-term care insurance by 2020. Mainland studies have found that long-term care insurance is the payer for less than 5% of long-term care costs. Many aging boomers may expect Medicaid to cover these costs.

Implications for Government

The data presented in this report suggest that Hawai`i state government will need to consider new ways of delivering and financing services as "baby boomers" becomes "senior boomers."

Several other state governments have begun looking at the implications of the coming senior boom in their states. For example, in Montana, data about their aging boomers were presented to various government offices. Potential implications for each Montana-government department were compiled in a report titled, The Aging Baby Boom: Implications for State Government, which provided a starting point for a listing of implications for Hawai`i government.

Given the expected diversity among the 18-year cohort of boomers, implications are discussed for two groups of aged boomers: 1) those who are healthy and active and 2) those who are disabled, frail, or vulnerable.

Healthy and Active Aged "Senior Boomers"

Hawai`i baby boomers are more likely to challenge the status quo and are used to having more independence than their parent's generation. Upon retirement, we can expect these boomers to continue to exercise their freedom of choice and to demand goods and services they believe are due them. This group of seniors will present challenges and opportunities in a number of areas of government responsibility and concern.

Labor and Industry. Labor force participation will likely decline as baby boomers retire, especially if two trends continue: 1) a net out-migration of workers in Hawai`i, which began in the 1990s and 2) the taking of early and/or partial retirement. This may have implications for:

- Retirement benefits for state retirees
- Employee retirement planning programs
- Availability of skilled individuals for jobs requiring high skill
- Part-time work opportunities for older adults
- Volunteer programs that utilize skills of retirees

Transportation. More older people will be on the road, both as drivers and as pedestrians, raising issues about driver and pedestrian safety. This may have implications for:

- Road building and maintenance, e.g., lighting, signs, crosswalks, curbs, speed limits and speed bumps, placement and timing of traffic lights
- Licensing, e.g, how and how often should older drivers be tested for fitness to drive?
- The routing, frequency, and cost of buses
- Other public transportation options

Taxation. Tax revenues will decrease if labor force participation declines. A greater proportion of tax payers will be older adults. These changes might call for:

- Changes in tax structures
- More tax-filing assistance programs

Education. More older people may want to attend school, while an aging population requires a work force that understands gerontology. This may have implications for:

- Educational offerings specifically for older adults
- The integration of older adults in campus classrooms
- Tuition assistance or waivers for older adults
- Training in gerontology for new students
- Continuing education in gerontology for mid-career individuals

Leisure Activities. More older people may want to attend senior clubs and will want public facilities to be senior-friendly. This may have implications for:

- Park and recreational facilities
- Organized activities specifically for older adults
- Libraries
- Entertainment facilities

Disabled, Frail, and Vulnerable "Senior Boomers"

Hawai`i baby boomers will live longer than their parent's generation, but greater proportions smoke, drink, and are overweight. They have smaller and more-scattered families, and many do not own homes. Many are not saving for retirement while, at the same time, the dependence ratio is increasing (meaning that fewer young people are available to work and contribute to the tax base that supports income-maintenance, health, and social service programs). Thus the number of elders who are disabled, frail, and vulnerable will increase, as the number of family and tax-dependent supports decrease. This group of seniors will present challenges to a number of areas of government responsibility and concern.

Income Maintenance. National studies suggest that boomers are not saving enough for retirement. Without reforms, Social Security benefits may need to be reduced to 75% of benefits due by 2030, resulting in a growing number of elders living in poverty or near poverty. This may have implication for:

- Income-maintenance programs such as SSI and Food Stamps
- Programs for the homeless

Transportation. A growing population of disabled, frail, or vulnerable older adults needs:

- More affordable transportation options for individuals with disabilities

- Safer streets, curbs, and crosswalks

Housing. A growing population of disabled, frail, or vulnerable older adults may have several implications for housing:

- Baby boomers who do not own their own home may need affordable housing options when they are seniors.
- Older adults with disabilities will need housing that can accommodate them and promote independent living.
- Older adults who are house-rich may benefit from reverse mortgage programs.
- Home-owners who become disabled may need help renovating their homes to promote independent living.
- As new living options for older adults are developed, standards and monitoring mechanisms will need to be developed.

Consumer Protection. People who are disabled, frail, and vulnerable are more easily victimized than people who are healthy. Increasing numbers of vulnerable elders may mean a higher prevalence of:

- Elder abuse, neglect, and financial exploitation in home settings
- Elder abuse and neglect in health and long-term care facilities
- Phone scams and con games
- Fraudulent and/or wasteful billing of Medicare and Medicaid
- New insurance products that need review and regulation

Prisons. Individuals who are imprisoned for life will age and die in prison. This may require:

- Disability-friendly prisons
- More health, social, and spiritual services in prisons
- Linkages with hospitals and nursing homes for care of older prisoners with these needs
- Medical parole programs

Health and Social Services. As the population ages, more of the users of government-sponsored health and social services will be elderly. More services may be needed for:

- Individuals with dementia (now 50% of elders 80 and older)
- Individuals with chronic conditions more common among those who smoke, drink, and are overweight (including heart disease, chronic obstructive pulmonary diseases, cancer, stroke, diabetes, and liver and kidney diseases)
- Individuals without family support
- Individuals with developmental disabilities who have aged
- Older adults with substance abuse problems
- Older adults with mental health needs

Long-Term Care. A growing population of disabled, frail, and vulnerable people will require an increase in home-based, community-based, and institutional long-term care services. This has implications for:

- Availability of long-term care services
- Licensing and monitoring of various long-term care services
- Public financing of long-term care
- Availability of a qualified elder-care work force

End-of-Life Care. A growing number of people dying of lingering, chronic conditions will require an increase in availability and funding for palliative care services. This has implications for:

- Availability of palliative services
- Licensing and monitoring of various palliative care services
- Public financing of palliative care and hospice
- Availability of a qualified palliative care work force

PART V
TECHNICAL APPENDIX

Demographic and Social Characteristics

Population

Table 1: Projected Hawai`i Resident Population, by Age and Sex: 2000, 2010 and 2020

Age Group	1995		2000		2010		2020	
	Total	Female	Total	Female	Total	Female	Total	Female
Total	1,179,198	583,389	1,238,501	614,410	1,366,770	679,928	1,494,144	743,277
< 5 years	95,196	46,268	90,094	43,482	97,148	46,863	106,056	51,175
5-9 years	84,715	41,127	92,738	45,688	90,193	44,212	100,854	49,401
10-14 years	81,292	39,333	82,566	40,022	87,033	42,810	94,085	46,170
15-19 years	78,763	38,206	81,192	38,947	91,612	44,895	88,958	43,370
20-24 years	82,042	36,695	96,011	42,967	100,005	44,616	104,571	47,429
25-29 years	81,253	38,433	82,414	39,279	100,408	46,980	110,826	52,932
30-34 years	95,360	46,303	76,733	37,325	94,237	45,459	98,134	47,098
35-39 years	100,803	49,096	93,545	45,439	78,409	38,377	96,078	46,031
40-44 years	96,139	47,166	98,467	48,224	75,219	36,708	92,379	44,785
45-49 years	81,043	40,270	93,184	46,311	90,393	44,639	75,544	37,679
50-54 years	61,460	31,328	79,013	39,522	94,296	47,027	71,814	35,795
55-59 years	47,337	25,265	60,429	31,121	89,900	45,359	87,458	43,825
60-64 years	45,103	23,897	47,156	25,412	77,519	39,554	92,268	46,835
65-69 years	47,660	25,888	43,400	23,339	58,670	30,916	86,259	44,430
70-74 years	41,404	21,706	44,054	24,528	42,771	23,841	70,071	36,839
75-79 years	29,106	15,577	36,134	19,490	35,518	20,020	48,632	26,665
80-84 years	17,199	9,203	23,088	12,903	31,055	18,408	30,681	18,111
85 years & older	13,323	7,628	18,283	10,411	32,384	19,244	39,476	24,707

Source: Hawai`i State Department of Business, Economic Development & Tourism. (1997). The State of Hawai`i Data Book 1997: A Statistical Abstract. Table 1.23.

49

Table 2: Population Estimates for Counties for Baby Boomers and Elderly Population: 1990 to 1998

		1990	1995	1996	1997	1998
Trailing-edge baby boomers (born 1956-64)	Hawai`i County	16,987	21,413	21,750	22,190	22,592
	Honolulu County	140,560	129,753	128,697	128,515	128,134
	Kaua`i County	7,650	8,543	8,742	8,762	8,819
	Maui County	16,550	19,239	19,734	20,003	20,233
	Total	181,747	178,948	178,923	179,470	179,778
Leading -edge baby boomers (born 1946-55)	Hawai`i County	21,468	21,449	21,102	20,971	20,707
	Honolulu County	131,692	130,340	129,110	128,607	126,903
	Kaua`i County	8,814	8,617	8,509	8,303	8,224
	Maui County	18,138	18,238	18,350	18,329	18,314
	Total	180,112	178,644	177,071	176,210	174,148
60 +	Hawai`i County	20,802	23,471	23,867	24,339	24,799
	Honolulu County	128,920	144,005	146,685	148,967	149,737
	Kaua`i County	8,919	9,647	9,956	10,045	10,160
	Maui County	15,621	17,741	18,068	18,275	18,558
	Total	174,262	194,864	198,576	201,626	203,254
65 +	Hawai`i County	15,066	17,830	18,339	18,775	19,124
	Honolulu County	91,913	110,487	113,934	116,325	116,950
	Kaua`i County	6,656	7,495	7,834	7,947	8,046
	Maui County	11,392	13,527	13,867	14,020	14,186
	Total	125,027	149,339	153,974	157,067	58,306
Total Population		1,112,772	1,183,066	1,187,283	1,192,057	1,193,001

Source: Hawai`i Department of Business, Economic Development & Tourism. (1997). The State of Hawai`i Data Book 1997, Statistical Abstract.
Note: Kalawao County is included in Maui County.

Table 3: Projection of Elderly Population 60+: United States vs. Hawai`i, 1995-2020 (Figure 1)

	1995	2000	2010	2020
U.S.	16.6% (43,593)*	16.5% (45,363)	18.7% (55,623)	22.9% (73,769)
Hawai`i	16.4% (193,795)	17.1% (212,115)	20.3% (277,917)	24.6% (367,387)

Source: 1. Administration on Aging. (1996-a). Retrieved August 13, 1999 from the Web:
       www.aoa.dhhs.gov/aoa/stats/proj1tbl.html
       2. Hawai`i Department of Business, Economic Development & Tourism. (1997). The State of Hawai`i
       Data Book 1997, Statistical Abstract.
Note: For U.S., the number is in thousands.

Table 4: Projection of Older Adults in Hawai`i (Figure 2)

	1990	2000	2010	2020
Older Adults 60+	15.7% (173,521)	17.1% (212,115)	20.3% (277,917)	24.6% (367,387)
65+	11.3% (124,677)	13.3% (164,959)	14.7% (200,398)	18.4% (275,119)
85+	1.0% (10,669)	1.5% (18,238)	2.4% (32,384)	2.6% (39,476)

Source: 1. Hawai`i Department of Business, Economic Development & Tourism. (1997). The State of Hawai`i
       Data Book 1997, Statistical Abstract.
       2. Hawai`i Executive Office on Aging. (1996). 2011 Project Briefing Book.

Table 5: Projection of Elderly 65+ in Hawai`i, Percentage of Elderly by Age Group, 1995-2020

Year	1995	2000	2010	2020
Total population Age 65+	148,692	164,959	200,398	275,119
65-69	32.0%	26.3%	29.3%	31.4%
70-74	27.8%	26.7%	21.3%	25.5%
75-79	19.6%	21.9%	17.7%	17.7%
80+	20.5%	25.1%	31.7%	25.5%

Source: Hawai`i Department of Business, Economic Development & Tourism. (1997). The State of Hawai`i
       Data Book 1997, Statistical Abstract.

Life Expectancy

Table 6: Life Expectancy at Birth by Sex for U.S. and Hawai`i: 1910-1990 and beyond

	Hawai`i			U.S.		
	Both Sexes	Male	Female	Both Sexes	Male	Female
1910	44.0	44.0	43.8	50.0	48.4	51.8
1920	45.7	45.6	45.8	54.1	53.6	54.6
1930	54.0	52.7	55.9	59.7	58.1	61.6
1940	62.0	59.9	64.9	62.9	60.8	65.2
1950	69.5	67.8	71.7	68.2	65.6	71.1
1960	72.4	70.4	74.8	69.7	66.6	73.1
1970	74.2	72.1	76.4	70.8	67.1	74.7
1980	77.8	74.5	81.5	73.7	70.0	77.4
1990	78.9	75.9	82.1	75.4	71.8	78.8
1995	N/A	N/A	N/A	N/A	72.5	79.3
2050	N/A	N/A	N/A	N/A	79.7	84.3

Source: 1. The HMSA Foundation. (1999). Health Trends in Hawai`i: A Profile of the Health Care System, Fourth Edition.
2. Administration on Aging. (1996-b). Retrieved August 13, 1999 from the Web: www.aoa.gov/aoa/stats/aging21/default.htm

Table 7: Hawai`i Life Expectancy at Birth by Ethnicity, 1910-1990, and by Sex and Ethnicity: 1990

Ethnicity	1910	1930	1950	1970	1990		
					Both Sexes	Male	Female
Caucasian	54.8	61.9	69.2	73.2	75.5	73.0	78.6
Chinese	54.2	60.1	69.7	76.1	82.9	79.8	86.1
Filipino	N/A	46.1	69.1	72.6	78.9	77.6	81.5
Hawaiian	32.6	41.9	62.5	67.6	74.3	71.5	77.2
Japanese	49.3	60.1	72.6	77.4	82.1	79.5	84.5
Other	15.6	32.6	68.3	76.7	80.4	78.1	82.6

Source: 1.   Hawai`i Department of Business, Economic Development & Tourism. (1997). The State of Hawai`i Data Book 1997, A Statistical Abstract, Table 2.10.
2. The HMSA Foundation (1999). Health Trends in Hawai`i: A Profile of the Health Care System, Fourth Edition.

Table 8: Projection of Life Expectancy at Age 65 in U.S.: 1980-2030 (Figure 3)

	1980	1979	2000	2010	2020	2030
Male	14.0	15.6	15.8	16.2	16.6	17.0
Female	18.4	19.2	19.3	19.6	20.0	20.4

Source: U.S. House of Representatives. (1998). Committee on Ways and Means, 1998 Green Book

Gender

Table 9: Projection of Sex Ratio of Older Adults 65+ and 85+: U.S. vs. Hawai`i (Figure 4)

	Male		Female		Sex Ratio	
Age 65+	US*	Hawai`i	US*	Hawai`i	US*	Hawai`i
1995	13678	68690	19866	80002	68.9	85.9
2000	14346	74288	20364	90671	70.4	81.9
2010	16887	87969	22522	112429	75.0	78.2
2020	23777	124367	29443	150752	80.8	82.5
2030	31718	NA	37661	NA	84.2	NA
Age 85+						
1995	1015	5695	2619	7628	38.8	74.6
2000	1228	7872	3031	10411	40.5	75.6
2010	1771	13140	3899	19244	45.4	68.3
2020	2141	14769	4319	24707	49.6	59.8
2030	3021	NA	5433	NA	55.6	NA

Source: 1. Administration on Aging. (1996-b). Retrieved August 13, 1999 from the Web:
www.aoa.gov/aoa/stats/aging21/default.htm
2. DBEDT (1997). The State of Hawai`i Data Book 1997: A Statistical Abstract
3. U.S. Census Bureau. (1998-b). The Statistical Abstract of the United States: 1998:The National Data Book

Note: * number in thousand
Sex ratio=number of males per 100 females.

Racial and Ethnic Diversity

Table 10: Racial Composition of Baby Boomers in 1990: U.S. vs. Hawai`i (Figure 5)

	White	Black	American Indian, Eskimo, Aleut	Asian or Pacific Islander	Other
United States	80.1 %	11.8 %	0.8 %	3.3 %	4.0 %
Hawai`i	38.2 %	2.8 %	0.5 %	56.5 %	2.0 %

Source: U.S. Bureau of Census. (1996-a). 1990 CPH-L-160. Retrieved August 18, 1999 from the Web:
www.census.gov/population/censusdata/cph-1-160h.txt

Table 11: Ethnic Composition of Baby Boomers in Hawai`i in 1990 (Figure 6)

Ethnicity	White	Black	Chinese	Filipino	Japanese	Korean	Hawaiian	Other Pacific Islander	Other
Percent	38.4%	2.9%	6.1%	13.8%	20.0%	2.4%	10.7%	3.7%	2.0%

Source: Hawai`i Executive Office on Aging. (1996). 2011 Project Briefing Book

Table 12: Race of Baby Boomers by Sex by County in Hawai`i

25-44 years old	Statewide	Hawai`i	Honolulu	Maui	Kaua`i
Both sexes					
White	146,678	18,014	104,374	16,982	7,308
Black	10,788	123	10,433	165	67
Asian or Pacific Islander	214,886	20,036	167,400	18,086	9,364
Other	9,520	1,146	7,069	830	475
All	381,872	39,319	289,276	36,063	17,214
Male					
White	80,024	9,250	58,078	8,979	3,717
Black	6,671	82	6,434	102	53
Asian or Pacific Islander	104,809	10,081	80,812	9,188	4,728
Other	5,206	559	3,892	498	257
All	196,710	19,972	149,216	18,767	8,755
Female					
White	66,654	8,764	46,296	8,003	3,591
Black	4,117	41	3,999	63	14
Asian or Pacific Islander	110,077	9,955	86,588	8,898	4,636
Other	4,314	587	3,177	332	14
All	185,162	19,347	140,060	17,296	8,459

Source: Hawai`i Executive Office on Aging. (1996). 2011 Project Briefing Book

Table 13: Hawai`i Crude Birth Rate per 1,000, by Ethnicity of Mother, 1990-1995

Ethnicity	1990	1991	1992	1993	1994	1995
Caucasian	20.5	19.0	18.1	17.3	16.7	15.2
Hawaiian	23.7	22.5	21.9	21.6	21.5	20.7
Chinese	11.0	11.1	10.3	10.4	9.9	10.1
Filipino	22.4	21.7	21.5	21.1	21.1	20.6
Japanese	9.7	9.3	9.1	8.6	9.1	8.3
Others	21.2	20.8	21.8	21.2	21.1	20.7

Source: The HMSA Foundation. (1999). Health Trends in Hawai`i: A Profile of the Health Care System. Fourth Edition.

Table 14: Immigrants Admitted, by Country of Birth: 1992-1996

Country of Birth	1992	1993	1994	1995	1996
All countries	7,885	8,504	7,746	7,537	8,436
Canada	180	220	155	167	125
Hong Kong	240	251	239	184	183
Japan	669	454	510	485	480
Korea	418	390	329	408	398
PR of China	528	745	743	480	555
Philippines	3,995	4,670	4,329	4,308	5,208
Taiwan	116	132	81	87	145
Vietnam	692	481	353	332	328
Other	1,047	1,161	1,007	1,086	1,014

Source: Hawai`i Department of Business, Economic Development & Tourism. (1997). The State of Hawai`i Data Book, 1997, Statistical Abstract.

Education

Table 15: Comparison of Educational Attainment of Baby Boomers in 1990, U.S. vs. Hawai`i (Figure 7)

	U.S.		Hawai`i	
Less than 9th grade	3,310,668	4.3 %	9,181	2.5 %
9th-12th grade, no diploma	8,330,706	10.8 %	23,588	6.5 %
High school graduate	22,574,815	29.3 %	97,078	26.8 %
Some college, no degree	17,132,710	22.3 %	92,809	25.6 %
Associates degree	6,443,130	8.4 %	40,595	11.2 %
Bachelor's degree	13,012,959	16.9 %	71,576	19.8 %
Graduate or professional degree	6,163,024	8.0 %	27,002	7.5 %
% of high school graduate	84.9 %		90.9 %	
% of bachelor's degree or higher	24.9 %		27.2 %	

Source: U.S. Bureau of Census. (1996-b). 1990 CPH-L-160. Retrieved August 18, 1999 from the Web:
   www.census.gov/population/censusdata/cph-1-160h.txt

Table 16: Years of School Completed by Persons 25 and Older: 1940-1990 (in percent)

	1940	1950	1960	1970	1980	1990
4 years of high school or more	20.5%	31.6%	46.1%	61.9%	73.8%	80.1%
4 years of college or more	5.3%	6.1%	9.0%	14.0%	20.3%	22.9%

Source: Hawai`i Department of Business, Economic Development & Tourism. (1997). The State of Hawai`i Data
   Book, 1997, Statistical Abstract.

Table 17: Educational Attainment by Gender: 1990 (in percent)

Educational Attainment	State Total
High School graduate or higher Male Female	 81.7% 78.4%
Bachelor's degree or higher Male Female	 24.4% 21.4%

Source: Hawai`i Department of Business, Economic Development & Tourism. (1997).
   The State of Hawai`i Data Book, 1997, Statistical Abstract.

Table 18: Educational Attainment by Race in Hawai`i in 1990 (in percent) (Figure 8)

	White	Black	American Indian, Eskimo, or Aleut	Asian or Pacific Islander	Other
Less than 9th grade	3.6%	1.3%	4.5%	13.9%	12.9%
9-12 grade	7.1%	4.5%	11.1%	11.3%	14.7%
HS graduate	24.4%	30.4%	26.0%	30.9%	34.3%
Some college	26.0%	40.4%	33.5%	16.2%	22.8%
Associate degree	8.7%	8.2%	7.3%	8.2%	6.3%
Bachelor's degree	18.8%	10.5%	10.1%	14.5%	6.6%
Graduate or Professional degree	11.4%	4.9%	7.5%	5.0%	2.4%

Source: Hawai`i Department of Economic and Business Development and Tourism. (1993). 1990 Census of Population and Housing, Hawai`i Data Disc, 1990 Population and Housing Summary Tape File 3A.

Table 19: Attainment of Degree & Certificate under UH Educational System, by Ethnicity: 1997

Ethnicity	Number	Percent
Caucasian	1,695	22 %
Japanese	1,572	21 %
Filipino	1,019	13 %
Chinese	784	10 %
Hawaiian/Part Hawaiian	777	10 %
Other	1,789	23 %

Source: Hawai`i Office of Hawaiian Affairs. (1998). Native Hawaiian Data Book, 1998

Table 20: Ability to Speak English among Ethnic Groups in Hawai`i: 1990

Ethnicity	Total Number responded	Speak English not well	Do not speak English	Total	Percent total of inability to speak English
Japanese	69,587	12,165	1,193	13,358	19%
Tagalog	55,341	8,701	652	9,353	17%
Ilocano	26,283	5,433	508	5,941	23%
Bisayan	1,710	340	14	354	21%
Chinese	25,489	5,476	1,508	2,084	8%
Korean	14,636	3,759	763	4,522	31%
Tongan	2,213	504	75	579	26%
Samoan	9,720	1,012	182	1,194	12%
Hawaiian	8,872	584	11	595	8%
Vietnamese	4,620	1,302	196	1,498	32%
Thai (Lao)	2,811	483	108	591	21%
French	3,825	270	0	270	7%
German	4,066	307	11	318	8%
Spanish	13,723	932	61	938	7%
Portuguese	1,110	89	0	89	8%

Source: Hawai`i Office of Hawaiian Affairs. (1998). Native Hawaiian Data Book, 1998

Marriage and Family

Table 21: Marital Status in Hawai`i: 1990

Marital Status	Both sex (n=870,203)	
	Number	Percentage
Never married	258,903	29.8%

Now married
    Leading edge boomer
    Trailing edge boomer
    65 years and above
	479,221
	120,983 (n=178,339)
	108,877 (n=200,696)
	53,771 (n=125,005)
		55.1%
		68%
		54%
		43%

Separated	13,964	1.6%
Widow	47,583	5.5%
Divorced	70,532	8.1%

Source: Hawai`i Department of Economic and Business Development and Tourism (1993). 1990
           Census of Population and Housing, Hawai`i Data Disc, Tape file 1A
           U.S. Census Bureau (1992). 1990 Census of Population. General Population
           Characteristics: Hawai`i, Series CP-1-13
Note: Marital status of people age 15 years old and above.

Table 22: Percent previously married among age 25-44: U.S. and Hawai`i between 1980-1990
(Figure 9)

	Age 25-29	Age 30-34	Age 35-44
US - Groom 1980 1990 US - Bride 1980 1990	 20.1% 13.8% 24.4% 19.9%	 21.9% 19.9% 20.6% 21.7%	 25.6% 33.8% 20.8% 31.3%
Hawai`i - Groom 1980 1990 Hawai`i - Bride 1980 1990	 14.5% 9.2% 24.9% 17.5%	 23.5% 18.4% 24.6% 23.5%	 30.5% 38.9% 22.5% 35.8%

Source: 1. Hawai`i Department of Health. Statistical Report 1980 and 1990.
       2. U.S. Census Bureau. (1998). Statistical Abstract of the United States 1998: The National Data Book

Table 23: Marital Status of elderly population age 65 +, U.S. 1995

	never married	ever married
U.S.	5.2%	94.8%
Hawai`i	2.7%	97.3%

Source: 1. Administration on Aging. (1996-b). Aging into the 21st Century. Retrieved August 13, 1999 from the Web: www.aoa.gob/aoa/aging21/default.htm

2. U.S. Department of Health and Human Services. Center for Disease Control. (1999). BRFSS. Retrieved January 25, 2000 from the Web: www2.cdc.gov/nccdphp/brfss/index.asp

Household and Living Arrangement

Table 24: Comparison of Households Characteristics of Baby Boomers between U.S. and Hawai`i in 1990

	Family Households			Non-family Households	
	Married couple	Male householder	Female householder	With others	Living alone
United States	58.9%	3.9%	13.5%	5.9%	17.8%
Hawai`i	59.6%	4.4%	10.3%	8.9%	16.9%

Source: U.S. BOC. (1996-b). Population and Housing Characteristics of Baby Boomers 26-44 years old: 1990. Retrieved August 18, 1999 from the Web: www.census.gov/population/censusdta/cph–160h.txt

Table 25: Percent of Living Alone Status of Older Adults in Hawai`i by County: 1990 (Figure 10)

Age	Sex	Statewide	Hawai`i	Honolulu	Maui	Kaua`i
Under 60 years old	Male	5.1%	5.9%	5.0%	5.9%	4.3%
	Female	3.7%	3.6%	3.8%	3.6%	2.7%
60 and older	Male	10.6%	12.5%	10.3%	11.4%	8.7%
	Female	19.4%	22.6%	22.8%	20.7%	21.2%
65 and older	Male	11.2%	13.1%	10.8%	12.2%	10.3%
	Female	22.6%	26.6%	27.6%	23.7%	25.9
85 and older	Male	16.6%	20.4%	15.2%	19.4%	19.6%
	Female	27.1%	27.6%	26.3%	28.4%	34.9%

Source: Executive Office on Aging, State of Hawai`i. (1998). The Hawai`i Data Book for Older Adults, 1998

Table 26: Projection of Older Adults Age 65 and Over Living Alone in US:1990-2020 (Figure 10)

	1990		2005		2020	
	Number	Percent	Number	Percent	Number	Percent
Total	9,176	31%	10,934	32%	15,220	31%
Male	1,943	16%	2,437	17%	3,604	17%
Female	7,233	42%	8,497	43%	11,616	42%
Race						
White	8,027	31%	9,087	33%	11,910	31%
Hispanic	226	22%	482	24%	930	25%
Black and others	925	30%	1,365	31%	2,381	32%

Source: Administration on Aging (1996-b). Aging into the 21st Century. Retrieved August 13, 1999 from the Web: www.aoa.gov/aoa/stats/aging21/default.htm

Note: Numbers in thousands. Percentage represent the number living alone out of the total in the class shown.

Interstate Mobility

Table 27: Residence in 1985: U.S. and Hawai`i (Figure 11)

	U.S.	Hawai`i
Lived in same house	31,559,511	136,699
Lived in different house in U.S.	43,288,007	203,883
Same State	34,180,552	127,387
Same county	24,954,121	117,479
Different county	9,226,431	9,908
Different state	9,107,455	76,496
Lived abroad	2,120,494	21,247

Source: U.S. Census Bureau (1996-b). Retrieved August 18, 1999 from the Web:
www.census.gov/population/censusdata/cph-1-160h.txt

Table 28: Interstate Movement of Job Seekers: 1950-1998 (Figure 12)

Year	Hawai`i workers on Mainland	Mainland workers in Hawai`i	Ratio
1950	966	1,105	114
1960	1,716	2,595	151
1970	5,078	6,062	119
1980	5,211	4,956	95
1990	5,275	2,910	55
1998	4,366	1,502	34

Source: Hawai`i Department of Business, Economic Development and Tourism (1998). The State of Hawai`i Data Book, 1998: A Statistical Abstract. Retrieved January 24, 2000 from the Web: www.state.hi.us./dbedt

Labor Force Participation and Economic Dependency

Table 29: Labor Force Participation of Baby Boomers in 1990: U.S. vs. Hawai`i

	Percent in labor force (Total)	Males	Females
U.S.	83.5 %	92.0 %	75.2 %
Hawai`i	86.5 %	93.2 %	79.5 %

Source: U.S. Census Bureau (1996-b). Retrieved August 18, 1999 from the Web:
www.census.gov/population/censusdata/cph-1-160h.txt

Table 30: Comparison of Female Labor Force Age between 25-44 : 1960 vs. 1990   (Figure 13)

	1960	1990
Female	32.1%	80%

Source: 1.   U.S. Department of Commerce, Bureau of Census. (1960). 1960 Census of Population, Volume 1, Characteristics of the Population Part 13, Hawai`i
2.   U.S. Bureau of Census (1996-b). Retrieved August 18, 1999 from the Web: www.census.gov/population/censusdata/cph-1-160h.txt

Table 31: Labor Force Profile in Hawai`i by Race: 1997

	Civilian Labor Force		Employed		
	Number	Percent	Number	Percent race	Percent total
Caucasian	193,000	32.6%	179,950	93.3%	32.4%
Japanese	145,850	24.8%	142,450	97.0%	25.7%
Filipino	97,150	16.4%	90,050	92.7%	16.3%
Hawaiian	67,700	11.4%	60,400	89.3%	10.9%
Chinese	38,950	6.6%	37,250	95.6%	6.7%
Korean	12,850	2.2%	12,100	93.8%	2.2%
Black	7,550	1.3%	6,850	90.7%	1.2%
American Indian/Eskimo/Aleut	2,850	0.5%	2,000	89.5%	0.5%
Other	25,100	4.2%	22,550	89.8%	4.1%
Total	592,000		554,150		

Source: Hawai`i Office of Hawaiian Affair. (1997). Native Hawaiian Data Book, 1997

Table 32: Projection of Unemployed Civilian Labor force in Hawai`i: 1990-2020

	1990	1995	2010	2020
Civilian Unemployed	2.8%	5.9%	5.1%	4.7%

Source: Hawai`i Department of Business, Economic Development and Tourism. (1996).
    Hawai`i Economy/Third Quarter 1996.

Table 33: The Trends of Retirement Age in U.S.: 1940-1995

	Age 62	Age 62-64	Age 65	Age 66+	Average age
1940	---	---	8.3%	91.7%	68.7
1950	---	---	23.1%	76.9%	68.5
1960	10.0 %	7.9%	35.3%	46.7%	66.2
1970	27.8%	23.2%	36.9%	12.1%	64.2
1980	40.5%	22.2%	30.7%	6.6%	63.7
1990	56.6%	20.2%	16.6%	6.7%	63.6
1995	58.3%	19.5%	16.3%	6.0%	63.6

Source: U.S. House of Representatives. (1998). Committee on Ways and Means, 1998 Green Book

Table 34: The projection of dependency and support ratios in Hawai`i: 1995-2020 (Figure 14)

Year	1995		2000		2010		2020	
	US	Hawai'i	US	Hawai'i	US	Hawai'i	US	Hawai`i
Dependency ratio (65+)	20.9%	21.5%	21.1%	22.7%	21.4%	25.7%	27.5%	30.0%
Support ratio (85+)	10.6%	8.7%	10.4%	9.8%	10.1%	12.4%	10.9%	15.7%

Source: 1. Friedland, & Summer, (1999). Demography Is Not Destiny. National Academy on an
        Aging Society.
    2. Hawai`i Department of Business, Economic Development & Tourism (1997). The State of Hawai`i Data
        Book, 1997, Statistical Abstract
    3. U.S. Census Bureau. (1999-c). Retrieved January 20, 1999 from the Web:
        www.census.gov/population/www/Projections/natdet-D1a.html

Income and Poverty

Table 35: Median Household and Family Income of Baby Boomers in 1989: U.S. vs. Hawai`i

	Hawai`i	United States
Median Household Income	$ 38,367	$ 34,601
Median Family Income	$40,079	$ 36,434
Median Nonfamily Household Income	$34,153	$ 29,275

Source: U.S. Bureau of Census (1996-b). Selected Social Characteristics of Baby Boomers, 26-44 years old in1990. Retrieved August 18, 1999 from the Web: www.census.gov/population/censusdata/cph-1-160h.txt.

Table 36: Poverty Status of Baby Boomers and Older Adults in Hawai`i by County in 1990

	Statewide	Hawai`i	Honolulu	Maui	Kaua`i
All persons whose poverty status is determined	1,071,352	118,344	803,204	99,344	50,460
Below poverty level	88,408	16,776	60,093	7,899	3,640
% Poverty	8.3%	14.2%	7.5%	8.0%	7.2%
Baby boomers (25-44) whose poverty status is determined	373,255	38,779	281,447	35,939	17,090
Below poverty level	25,610	5,001	17,136	2,494	979
% poverty	6.9%	12.9%	6.1%	6.9%	5.7%
Older adults (65+) whose poverty status is determined	169,535	20,659	124,859	15,416	8,601
Below poverty level	19,204	3,090	13,320	1,704	1,090
% poverty	11.3%	15.0%	10.7%	11.1%	12.7%
Older adults (75+) whose poverty status is determined	42,359	5,406	30,481	3,894	2,578
Below poverty level	7,072	1,073	4,725	757	517
% poverty	16.7%	19.8%	15.5%	19.4%	20.1%

Source: Hawai`i Executive Office on Aging. (1996). 2011 Project Briefing Book

Table 37: Percentage of Adults 65+ in Poverty and Near Poverty by Race/Ethnicity in U.S.1996

	Poor	Near Poor	Total
All races	10.8%	7.6%	18.4%
Non-Hispanic White	9.4%	7.3%	16.7%
Black	25.3%	11.4%	36.7%
Asian/Pacific Islander	9.7%	4.6%	14.3%
Hispanic	24.4%	11.9%	36.3%

Source: Yung-Ping Chen (1999). Racial Disparity in Retirement Income Security: Directions for Policy Reform. In Toni P. Miles (Ed.), Full-Color Aging: Facts, Goals, and Recommendations for America's Diverse Elders (pp.21-31). Washington, DC: The Gerontological Society of America.

Table 38: Percentage of Adults 60+ in Low Income Status in Hawai`i by Race and by County 1989

	Statewide	Hawai`i	Honolulu	Maui	Kaua`i
Non Hispanic White	12.0%	16.8%	11.1%	10.4%	12.0%
Minority	11.1%	14.0%	10.5%	11.4%	12.9%

Source: Hawai`i Executive Office on Aging. (1998). The Hawai`i Data Book for Older Adults 1(1998)

Social Security and Pension

Table 39: Adults 65+ with Social Security, Retirement Income, and Earnings in Hawai`i by County 1989

| County | Noninstitutionalized person 65 and over | | | | | | | | | | | |
| | With SS income | | No SS income | | With retirement income | | No retirement income | | With Earnings | | No Earnings | |
	#	%	#	%	#	%	#	%	#	%	#	%
Statewide	96,765	80.0	24,214	20.0	48,182	39.8	72,797	60.2	28,125	23.2	92,854	76.8
Hawai`i	12,782	86.5	1,992	13.5	5,708	38.6	9,066	61.4	3,297	22.3	11,477	77.7
Honolulu	69,135	78.0	19,476	22.0	35,576	40.1	53,035	59.9	20,681	23.3	67,930	76.7
Maui	9,415	84.8	1,683	15.2	4,255	38.3	6,843	61.7	2,695	24.3	8,403	75.7
Kaua`i	5,433	83.6	1,063	16.4	2,643	40.7	3,853	59.3	1,452	22.4	5,044	77.6

Source: Hawai`i Executive Office on Aging. (1998). The Hawai`i Data Book for Older Adults, 1998

Table 40: Shares of Income by Quantiles of Total Income of Elders 1996

Source	Lowest	Second	Third	Fourth	Highest
Social Security	81%	80%	66%	47%	21%
Pensions	3%	7%	15%	24%	21%
Asset income	3%	6%	9%	15%	25%
Earnings	1%	3%	7%	12%	31%
Public Assistance	11%	2%	1%	< 0.5%	< 0.5%
Other income	1%	2%	3%	2%	2%

Source: Yung-Ping Chen (1994). Racial Disparity in Retirement Income Security: Directions for Policy Reform. In Toni P. Miles (Ed.), Full-Color Aging: Facts, Goals, and Recommendations for America's Diverse Elders (pp.21-31). Washington, DC: The Gerontological Society of America.

Table 41: Pension Sponsorship, Participation, Vesting Among Civilian, Nonagricultural Wage and Salary Workers, Aged 16 and over, in the U.S.1993

	Total Workers (thousands)	Sponsorship Rate	Participation Rate	Sponsored Participation Rate	Vesting Rate	Participant Vesting Rate
Total	105,815	62.1%	47.1%	75.9%	40.3%	85.5%
Age: 16-20	6,634	32.2%	3.5%	11.0%	1.6%	45.6%
21-30	26,359	56.6%	33.8%	59.8%	25.8%	76.2%
31-40	31,047	65.8%	52.7%	80.1%	45.0%	85.3%
41-50	23,459	70.6%	61.5%	87.1%	54.5%	88.7%
51-60	13,164	66.8%	59.3%	88.8%	53.3%	89.9%
61-64	2,781	62.4%	51.3%	82.3%	47.7%	92.9%
65+	2,371	46.1%	29.0%	63.0%	26.6%	91.6%
Sex:						
Male	55,582	62.3%	50.0%	80.2%	42.8%	85.6%
Female	50,233	61.8%	44.0%	71.2%	37.6%	85.3%
Race:						
White	90,654	62.2%	47.7%	76.6%	41.0%	86.1%
Black	11,622	62.7%	45.3%	72.3%	36.8%	81.3%
Other	3,539	57.1%	40.1%	70.2%	32.7%	81.7%
Annual Earnings:						
Less than $5,000	2,207	29.3%	3.0%	10.3%	2.2%	71.2%
$5,000-10,000	4,261	39.5%	12.9%	32.8%	9.8%	75.5%
$10,001-14,999	7,657	48.7%	29.3%	60.1%	22.2%	75.8%
$15,000-19,999	9,349	62.7%	45.2%	72.0%	36.1%	79.9%
$20,000-24,000	9,403	73.4%	60.6%	82.6%	51.7%	85.2%
$25,000-29,999	7,620	75.6%	64.4%	85.2%	54.5%	84.6%
$30,000-49,999	16,949	82.6%	75.1%	90.9%	67.0%	89.2%
$50,000 or more	7,542	85.2%	79.6%	93.5%	73.4%	92.2%
Industry:						
Federal gov't	3,268	90.0%	79.0%	87.7%	70.4%	89.2%
State/local gov't	15,228	89.3%	74.4%	83.3%	66.0%	88.7%
Mining	648	73.3%	66.9%	91.3%	60.0%	90.2%
Construction	4,868	35.4%	29.7%	84.0%	25.2%	84.8%
Manufacturing:						
Nondurables	8,095	68.2%	55.5%	81.3%	45.8%	82.5%
Durables	10,714	76.5%	63.5%	83.0%	54.9%	86.5%
Transportation	4,064	60.4%	47.0%	77.8%	39.0%	83.1%
Communications, utilities	2,426	89.0%	77.9%	87.5%	69.7%	89.4%
Wholesale trade	4,426	56.6%	45.4%	80.3%	38.2%	84.1%
Retail trade	18,175	42.2%	24.1%	57.0%	19.3%	80.0%
Finance, real estate, insurance	6,927	70.4%	52.6%	74.7%	45.6%	86.7%
Business, personal entertainment	10,629	30.3%	19.0%	62.8%	15.8%	83.0%
Professional srvs	16,346	63.2%	42.5%	67.3%	35.3%	83.1%

Source: Yakoboski, P. & Silverman, C. (1994). Baby boomers in retirement: What are their prospects? EBRI Issue Brief (151):1-42.

Savings and Assets

Table 42: Tenure of Housing by Baby Boomers, U.S. vs. Hawai`i in 1990 (Figure 15)

	Owner occupied	Renter occupied
U.S.	57.1 percent	42.9 percent
Hawai`i	41.4 percent	58.6 percent

Source: U.S. Bureau of Census (1996-a). Retrieved August 18, 1999 from the Web:
www.census.gov/population/censusdata/cph-1-160h.txt

Table 43: Home Ownership of Older Adults in Hawai`i by age group (Figure 16)

Age group	Owner occupied	Percentage	Renter occupied	Percentage
All 60 and older	72,643	72.1	28,102	27.9
60 to 64	19,353	72.8	7,248	27.2
65 to 74	34,537	74.0	12,118	26.0
75 to 84	15,523	69.5	6,828	30.5
85 and older	3,230	62.9	1,908	37.1

Source: Hawai`i Executive Office on Aging (1998).  The Hawai`i Data Book for Older Adults, 1998

Table 44: Home Ownership of Older Adults by County in Hawai`i (in percent)

Age group	State	Honolulu	Hawai`i	Maui	Kaua`i
All 60 and older	72.1	70.0	78.4	77.6	76.2
60 to 64	72.8	71.0	78.9	78.9	77.1
65 to 74	74.0	71.6	81.2	80.3	79.4
75 to 84	69.5	67.5	74.9	73.1	72.4
85 and older	62.9	59.8	74.1	63.8	69.4

Source: Hawai`i Executive Office on Aging. (1998).  The Hawai`i Data Book for Older Adults, 1998

Table 45: Tenure of Housing and the Average Cost of Mortgage in Hawai`i: 1992-1997

	Year	Statewide	Honolulu	Hawai`i	Maui	Kaua`i
Home owner	1992	51.9%	47.6%	67.8%	61.0%	59.9%
	1997	57.9%	53.8%	72.3%	65.0%	67.1%
Average monthly mortgage	1992	$ 800	$821	$651	$776	$720
	1997	$1,319	$1,430	$954	$1,210	$1,151

Source: Hawai`i Housing Policy Study (1999). Retrieved January 25, 2000 from the Web:
www.hcdch.state.hi.us/hsgstats.html

Health and Long-Term Care

Health Behavior

Table 46: Percentage Estimated Prevalence of Behavior Risk Factors: U.S. vs. Hawai`i

United States	1991			1993			1995			1997		
	Total	Men	Women	Total	Men	Women	Total	Men	Women	Total	Men	Women
Cigarette Smoking	25.4	25.1	21.3	22.2	23.6	20.6	22.4	24.7	20.9	23.2	25.4	21.1
Alcohol Binge Drinking	NA	21.7	6.5	14.2	21.1	7.3	14.1	21.6	7.0	14.5	22.3	6.8
Alcohol Chronic Drinking	NA	6.1	0.9	3.0	5.4	0.8	2.8	5.0	0.8	3.0	5.3	0.8
Seat Belt Use	76.2	NA	NA	79.3	NA	NA	67.0	59.0	74.0	69.5	61.9	74.8
Overweight	27.8	NA	NA	30.1	NA	NA	NA	NA	NA	31.1	32.1	29.4
Hawai`i												
Cigarette Smoking	20.1	23.8	16.5	18.7	19.7	17.8	17.8	18.8	16.8	18.7	21.5	15.8
Alcohol Binge Drinking	17.1	27.2	7.3	15.1	25.2	5.2	12.4	21.0	3.9	17.1	27.3	6.8
Alcohol Chronic Drinking	5.4	9.9	0.9	5.0	9.1	1.0	2.9	4.7	1.0	5.0	8.5	1.4
Seat Belt Use	96.0	NA	NA	96.1	NA	NA	95.4	NA	NA	87.2	84.0	90.5
Overweight	24.0	NA	NA	24.0	NA	NA	21.8	NA	NA	26.6	28.4	24.7

Source: 1. The HMSA Foundation (1999). Health Trends in Hawai`i: A Profile of the Health Care System. Fourth Edition. For 1991, 1993, and 1995

2. U.S. Department of Health and Human Services. Center for Disease Control and Prevention (1997). Retrieved January 25, 2000 from the Web: www.cdc.gov/nccdphp/brfss/index.asp.

Table 47: Health Risks and Lifestyle of Baby Boomers in Hawai`i: 1990 (Figure 17)

Risk Factor	Baby Boomers		Leading Edge BB		Trailing Edge BB	
	US	Hawai`i	US	Hawai`i	US	Hawai`i
Cigarette Smoking	22.3%	20.2%	16.7%	15.7%	27.2%	23.2%
Acute Drinking	8.2%	14.0%	3.6%	8.9%	12.3%	17.4%
Alcohol Chronic Drinking	2.4%	5.2%	1.8%	5.3%	3.0%	5.1%
Obesity	30.8%	23.7%	32.2%	21.9%	29.7%	24.9%
Overweight	26.1%	20.1%	26.8%	17.7%	25.5%	21.8%
Seat Belt Use	73.1%	95.8%	72.5%	96.2%	73.7%	95.5%

Source: U.S. Department of Health and Human Services (1996). National Center for Chronic Disease Prevention and Health Promotion, Behavioral Surveillance Branch CD-ROM Series 1, No.1, Behavioral Risk Factor Surveillance System 1984-1995 Survey Data.

Table 48: Health Risks and Lifestyle of Baby Boomers in Hawai`i: 1997-1998 (Figure 18)

Risk Factor	Baby Boomers	Leading-edge Boomers	Trailing-edge Boomers	Male	Female
Cigarette Smoking	21.0%	21.1%	19.5%	22.7%	18.0%
Acute Drinking	19.2%	19.8%	21.2%	32.1%	8.3%
Overweight	32.5%	36.6%	33.6%	40.1%	30.1%
Diabetes	2.3%	5.2%	3.0%	3.5%	4.6%
Poor Health Status	1.3%	1.3%	0.7%	0.8%	1.2%
Physically inactive	19.6%	20.7%	20.9%	16.5%	25.0%
Not regular & sustained leisure time physical activity	74.2%	74.1%	77.5%	78.4%	73.3%

Source: Hawai`i Department of Health. (1999). 1996-1998 Hawai`i Behavioral Risk Factor Surveillance System Results. Health Surveys and disease Registry Section, Office of Health Status Monitoring. Honolulu, HI.

Table 49: Comparison of Selected Health Risks of Older Adults age 65 and above: U.S. vs. Hawai`i 1997-1998

	Diabetes	Hypertension	At risk for overweight related problem	At risk of smoke related problem	At risk of lack of exercise related problem
U.S.	12.5%	46.2%	32.1%	11.1%	80.3%
Hawai`i	16.6%	45.1%	28.1%	7.1%	62.4%

Source: U.S. Department of Health and Human Services. Center for Disease Control and Prevention. (1997). Retrieved January 25, 2000 from the Web: www.cdc.gov/nccdphp/brfss/index.asp.

Prevalence of Major Diseases/Chronic Condition

Table 50: Cancer Incidence by Sex and Specified Site: 1990-1994 (per 100,000 population)

	All cases		Colon		Lung		Prostate	Breast
	Male	Female	Male	Female	Male	Female	Male	Female
U.S.	485.1	342.4	39.0	27.4	79.5	42.0	151.7	108.2
Hawai`i	425.7	309.8	39.3	27.4	63.8	31.4	122.7	99.2

Source: The HMSA Foundation. (1999). Health Trends in Hawai`i: A Profile of the Health Care System. Fourth Edition.

Table 51: Prevalence of Selected Chronic Conditions of People by Age Group in Hawai`i: 1998 (per 1,000 person)

	Age 35-44		Age 45-54		Age 55-64		Age 65-74		Age 75+	
	Male	Female	Male	Female	Male	Female	Male	Female	Male	Female
Arthritis	28.6	41.5	62.9	123.4	117.7	224.9	164.2	340.3	225.2	393.2
Asthma	58.1	86.7	69.1	85.3	70.6	69.0	32.5	73.0	66.1	66.6
Diabetes	21.1	36.0	85.5	69.3	122.8	131.1	151.1	121.9	116.9	134.3
Hypertension	105.3	77.0	235.8	187.9	313.0	301.7	370.4	390.9	377.1	393.4

Source: Hawai`i Department of Health, Office of health status Monitoring, HHS (1998). Retrieved December 20, 1999 from the Web www.state.hi.us/doh/stats/surveys/hs-hsp.html

Table 52: Prevalence of Selected Chronic Conditions Per 1,000 Persons by Ethnicity in Hawai`i 1998

	Caucasian	Hawaiian	Chinese	Filipino	Japanese	Others	Total
Arthritis	95.9	51.7	90.7	65.3	80.1	66.1	84,301
Asthma	63.7	148.2	78.2	80.0	78.6	73.4	102,533
Diabetes	27.2	47.0	35.3	45.9	63.5	48.7	52,997
Hypertension	105.8	102.7	142.8	151.1	186.7	94.9	149,465

Source: Hawai`i Department of Health. Office of Health Status Monitoring, HHS (1998). Retrieved December 20, 1999 from the Web www.state.hi.us/doh/stats/surveys/hs-hsp.html

Leading Causes of Death

Table 53: Death Rates by Leading Causes for All Ages between U.S. and Hawai`i 1995 (per 100,000 population) (Figure 19)

Disease	U.S.	Hawai`i
Heart disease	280.7	196.0
Malignant neoplasms	204.9	156.4
Cerebrovascular diseases	60.1	51.5
Chronic obstructive pulmonary diseases	39.2	20.4
Pneumonia, flu	31.6	NA
Chronic liver diseases, cirrhosis	9.6	NA
Suicide	11.9	12.0
Homicide	NA	4.9
Accidents including motor vehicle accidents	35.1	39.6
Diabetes Mellitus	NA	14.2

Source: U.S. Department of Commerce (1998). Economics and Statistics Administration, Bureau of the Census, Statistical Abstract of the United States 1998: The National Data Book

Table 54: Selected Leading Causes of Death in Hawai`i among people age 25-44: 1950-1996

	1950 (N=311)	1960 (N=304)	1980 (N=384)	1996 (N=533)
Heart Disease	16.4%	21.4%	16.7%	15.0%
Cancer & malignant Neoplasms	15.7%	24.0%	16.7%	18.4%
TB	9.0%	NA	0.0%	NA
Accident	6.4%	16.8%	24.2%	NA
Motor Vehicle Accident	5.5%	6.3%	13.5%	8.9%
Suicide	5.8%	4.3%	11.5%	10.1%

Source: 1. Board of Health, Territory of Hawai`i, Annual Report 1950, Hawai`i Department of Health, Statistical Report 1960 and 1980; Vital Statistics 1996.

Note: NA, not available or classification is different from the previous years.

Table 55: Hawai`i Death Rates (per 100,000) by Causes of Death by Age Group in 1997

Disease	Age Group				
	0-14	15-24	25-44	45-64	65+
Atherosclerosis	0.0	0.0	0.0	0.4	6.4
Cerebrovascular disease	0.8	1.8	5.6	31.9	368.9
Congenital Anomaly	11.0	0.6	0.8	1.2	1.3
COPD	0.0	1.8	2.2	10.0	135.9
Diabetes Mellitus	0.0	0.6	1.1	23.9	83.0
Heart Disease	2.4	6.1	20.0	148.2	1178.7
HIV infection	0.0	0.0	6.1	5.6	1.3
Influenza/Pneumonia	0.4	1.2	1.9	9.6	206.8
Liver Disease	0.0	0.0	3.1	8.8	16.6
Malignant Neoplasm	4.3	2.4	22.0	168.5	818.1
Nephritis	0.4	0.0	1.1	6.0	44.0
Perinatal Condition	17.7	0.0	0.0	0.0	0.6
Septicemia	0.4	0.6	1.1	6.0	53.0
Suicide	0.8	6.7	16.7	18.3	8.3
Symptoms/ill-defined	3.1	0.0	1.1	3.2	30.0
Accidents:motor vehicles & unintentional injury	6.7	22.5	24.3	24.3	65.7
Others	9.8	14.6	25.1	69.3	585.2

Source: The HMSA Foundation. (1999) . Health Trends in Hawai`i: A Profile of the Health Care System. Fourth Edition.

Table 56: Comparison of Selected Leading Causes of Death of people 65+ 1950-1996

Disease	1950 (n=1145)	1980 (n=2905)	1996 (n=5657)
Cerebrovascular disease	12.0%	10.5%	9.1%
Diabetes Mellitus	3.9%	2.8%	2.6%
Heart Disease	43.5%	38.6%	33.6%
Influenza/Pneumonia	3.8%	5.2%	5.4%
Malignant Neoplasm	16.8%	21.7%	22.3%
Suicide	0.9%	0.5%	0.2%
TB	1.8%	0.4%	NA

Source: Territory of Hawai`i, Board of Health, Annual Report 1950; Statistical Report 1980; Vital Statistics 1996
Disability rates and Nursing Home Population:

Table 57: Projection of Persons with Limitations in Activity in the United States, 1994-2040

Year	All Ages (in Thousands)	Under 65 years	65 Years and older - Total	65-74 years	75 years and older
1994	39,057	27,211	11,846	6,215	5,631
2000	43,562	29,648	13,914	6,315	7,599
2010	49,759	33,749	16,010	7,145	8,865
2020	56,011	35,116	20,895	10,529	10,366
2030	62,738	35,204	27,534	12,942	14,592
2040	68,592	37,114	31,478	11,573	19,905

Source: Rice, D.P. (1996). Beneficiary profile: Yesterday, today, and tomorrow. Health Care Financing Review 18(2):23-45.

Table 58: Summary of Projections of Disabled Elderly Population in U.S.

Disabled Elderly Population (in millions)	Source	Baseline		Future	
		Year	Population	Year	Population
Total Disabled Elderly	A	1985	6.8 million	2060	14-24 million
	B	1990	11.1 million	2030	23-27 million
Disabled in a nursing home	A	1985	1.3 million	2060	3-5 million
	B	1990	1.8 million	2030	4-5 million
Disabled in community	A	1985	5.5 million	2060	11-18 million
	B	1990	9.2 million	2030	19-22 million
Using Long-Term care	C	1988	6.3 million	2018	9-13 million
Using home care	C	1988	4.0 million	2018	6-8 million

Source: U.S. Senate. (1991). Long-term care: Projected needs of the aging baby boom generation. Report to the Honorable William S. Cohen, Special Committee on Aging. Washington, D.C.: General Accounting Office, GAO/HRD-91-86

Table 59: Average Occupancy Rate of Long-Term Care Facilities in Hawai`i 1991-1998 (Figure 21)

	1991	1992	1993	1994	1995	1996	1997	1998
Rates	93.4%	96.2%	95.9%	97.8%	94.4%	92.3%	90.7%	90.5%

Source: 1. Hawai`i State Health Planing and Development Agency. (1999). Long-term care List 1998. Honolulu, HI.:Author
2. Healthcare Association of Hawai`i. (1997).  Hawai`i Long-term care Facility Data Trends: 1991-1995.

Health and Long-Term Care Insurance

Table 60: Health Insurance Status and Type of Coverage in U.S. 1998

United States	Uninsured	Insured	Private plan	Employment based	Government	Medicare	Medicaid	Military
Number	44,281	227,462	190,861	168,576	66,087	35,887	27,854	8,747
Percent	16.3%	83.7%	70.2%	62.0%	24.3%	13.2%	10.3%	3.2%

Source: U.S. Census Bureau. (1999). Health Insurance Coverage: 1998. Retrieved October 15, 1999 from the Web www.census.gov

Note: The estimates by type of coverage are not mutually exclusive; people can be covered by more than one type of health insurance during the year.

Table 61: Uninsured People Age 35-54 in Hawai`i 1998

	Honolulu		Hawai`i		Kaua`i		Maui		Total	
Age:	Number	%	Number	%	Number	%	Number	%	Number	%
Age 35-44	9,205	7	2,494	10	954	10	2,235	10	14,888	8
Age 45-54	5,979	5	1,692	9	829	11	1,880	12	10,379	7
Race:										
Caucasian	10,661	7	3,021	9	2,004	16	4,414	14	20,101	9
Hawaiian	10,455	7	2,947	7	1,004	9	2,123	8	16,538	7
Chinese	2,585	5	214*	10*	NA	NA	78	4	2,877	5
Filipino	5,777	4	1,538	8	390	3	1,224	6	8,930	5
Japanese	4,548	2	1,178	5	305	3	296	2	6,327	3
Other	13,344	9	2,535	13	984	11	2,727	14	19,590	10
Total	47,369	6	11,433	8	4,687	8	10,873	0	74,362	6

Source: Hawai`i Department of Health., Office of Health Status Monitoring. (1998). Retrieved December 20, 1999 from the Web www.state.hi.us/doh/stats/surveys/hs-hsp.html.

Table 62: Health Insurance Status and Type of Coverage of Baby Boomers in Hawai`i: 1998

	Insured	Your employer	Someone else's employer	Self-bought plan	Medicaid or Medical assistance	Military, CHAMPUS or VA	Other
Baby boomers	92.0%	63.6%	19.6%	6.5%	5.3%	4.8%	0.4%
Leading edge boomers	90.7%	63.5%	22.7%	5.2%	5.4%	2.6%	0.6%
Trailing edge boomers	93.4%	61.3%	18.4%	4.0%	5.0%	10.9%	0.4%

Source: Hawai`i Department of Health. (1999).  1996-1998 Hawai`i Behavioral Risk Factor Surveillance System Results. Health Survey and Disease Registry Section, Office of Health Status Monitoring, Honolulu, HI.

Health and Long-term care Expenditures

Table 63: National Health Expenditures aggregate and per capita amounts, percent distribution, and average annual percent growth, by source of funds in U.S 1990-2030 (Figure 20)

Item	1990	2000	2010	2020	2030
National health expenditure (percent of GDP)	12.1%	18.1%	22.0%	26.5%	32.0%
National health expenditures (amount in billions)	$ 666.2	$1,739.8	$3,787.8	$7,839.4	$15,969.6
Private	383.6	859.9	1,819.2	3,776.1	7,753.0
Public	282.6	879.9	1,968.6	4,063.2	8,216.7
Federal	195.4	617.5	1,448.4	3,074.5	6,321.0
State and local	87.3	262.4	520.2	988.7	1,895.6
U.S. population	259.6	283.0	302.5	320.3	333.5
National health expenditures (per capita amount) Private	$ 2,566	$ 6,148	$12,522	$24,478	$47,891
Public	1,478	3,039	6,014	11,791	23,250
Federal	1,089	3,109	6,508	12,687	24,641
State and local	753	2,182	4,788	9,600	18,956
	336	927	1,720	3,087	5,685
National health expenditure (percent distribution)	100.0%	100.0%	100.0%	100.0%	100.0%
Private	57.6%	49.4%	48.0%	48.2%	48.5%
Public	42.4%	50.6%	52.0%	51.8%	51.5%
Federal	29.3%	38.2%	38.2%	39.2%	39.6%
State and local	13.1%	13.7%	13.7%	12.6%	11.9%

Source: Burner, S.T., Waldo, D.R., & McKusick, D.R. (1992). National health expenditures projections through 2030. Health Care Financing Review 14(1): 1-29

Table 64: Percent Distribution of National Health Expenditures, by source of funds and type of expenditure: United States, 1990-2030 (Figure 20)

Type of expenditure 1990 ($666.2 billion)	Total	Private					Government		
		All Private	Consumer			Other	Total	Federal	State & local
			Total	Out of Pocket	Private Insurance				
National health expenditure	$666.2	57.6%	53.0%	20.4%	32.5%	4.6%	42.4%	29.3%	13.1%
Health services & supplies	643.4	58.2%	54.9%	21.2%	33.7%	3.4%	41.8%	28.7%	13.1%
Personal health care	585.3	58.7%	55.1%	23.3%	31.8%	3.6%	41.3%	30.3%	11.0%
Hospital care	256.0	45.3%	39.9%	5.0%	34.9%	5.4%	54.7%	40.9%	13.8%
Physician service	125.7	65.0%	65.0%	18.7%	46.3%	0.0%	35.0%	28.0%	7.0%
Dental services	34.0	97.5%	97.5%	53.0%	44.5%	---	2.3%	1.1%	1.1%
Other prof service	31.6	79.6%	68.1%	27.7%	40.4%	11.5%	20.4%	15.5%	4.9%
Home health care	6.9	26.5%	19.4%	12.1%	7.3%	7.1%	73.5%	58.6%	14.9%
Drugs/other non-durables	54.6	88.9%	88.9%	73.6%	15.3%	---	11.3%	5.6%	5.6%
Vision products/other medical durables	12.1	77.7%	77.7%	67.4%	10.4%	---	22.3%	19.5%	2.8%
Nursing home care	53.1	47.9%	46.0%	44.9%	1.1%	1.9%	52.1%	32.3%	19.8%
Other personal hlth care	11.3	19.9%	---	---	---	19.9%	80.1%	48.7%	31.3%
Program admin & net cost of private health insurance	38.7	80.7%	79.2%	---	79.2%	1.4%	19.3%	12.3%	7.0%
Government public health activities	19.3	---	---	---	---	---	100%	12.1%	87.9%
Research and construction	22.8	38.6%	---	---	---	38.6%	61.4%	48.3%	13.1%

Table 64 (continued)									
Type of expenditure	Total	Private					Government		
2000 ($1,739.8 billions)		All Private	Consumer Total	Out of Pocket	Private Insurance	Other	Total	Federal	State & local
National health expenditure	$1,739.8	49.4%	45.7%	17.4%	28.3%	3.8%	50.6%	35.5%	15.1%
Hlth services & supplies	1,696.4	49.9%	46.8%	17.8%	29.0%	3.0%	50.1%	35.0%	15.2%
Personal health care	1,572.1	49.6%	46.4%	19.3%	27.1%	3.2%	50.4%	36.7%	13.7%
Hospital care	701.2	38.2%	33.5%	4.1%	29.5%	4.6%	61.8%	45.7%	16.1%
Physician service	344.8	56.5%	56.5%	16.4%	40.1%	0.0%	43.5%	35.9%	7.5%
Dental services	62.3	95.7%	95.7%	52.6%	43.1%	---	4.3%	2.4%	1.9%
Other prof service	82.5	70.2%	60.0%	23.4%	36.6%	10.1%	29.8%	21.7%	8.1%
Home health care	30.5	18.3%	13.4%	8.2%	5.2%	4.9%	81.7%	57.6%	24.1%
Drugs/non-durables	125.5	82.7%	82.7%	67.2%	15.5%	---	17.3%	9.3%	8.0%
Vision products/other medical durables	24.2	72.0%	72.0%	63.4%	8.6%	---	28.0%	25.5%	2.6%
Nursing home care	147.0	46.0%	44.2%	43.1%	1.1%	1.8%	54.0%	32.7%	21.3%
Oth personal hlth care	54.1	9.5%	---	---	---	9.5%	90.5%	53.5%	37.0%
Program admin & net cost of private health insurance	84.5	78.5%	77.1%	---	77.1%	1.4%	21.5%	13.4%	8.0%
Government public health activities	39.9	---	---	---	---	---	100%	13.3%	86.7%
Research and construction	43.4	32.1%	---	---	---	32.1%	67.9%	56.2%	11.6%

Source: Burner, S.T., Waldo, D.R., & McKusick, D.R. (1992). National health expenditures projections through 2030 Health Care Financing Review, (14): 1, pp.1-29

Table 64 (continued)									
Type of expenditure	Total	Private					Government		
2010 ($3,787.8 billion)		All Private	Consumer			Other	Total	Federal	State & local
			Total	Out of Pocket	Private Insurance				
National expenditure	$3,787.8	48.0%	44.4%	16.4%	28.0%	3.6%	52.0%	38.2%	13.7%
Health services/supplies	3,707.4	48.4%	45.4%	16.8%	28.6%	3.0%	51.6%	37.8%	13.8%
Personal health care	3,457.7	47.7%	44.6%	18.0%	26.6%	3.1%	52.3%	39.6%	12.6%
Hospital care	1,551.5	38.4%	33.7%	4.1%	29.6%	4.6%	61.6%	47.2%	14.4%
Physician service	848.4	50.1%	50.1%	14.6%	35.5%	0.0%	49.9%	43.3%	6.6%
Dental services	104.7	95.5%	95.5%	52.7%	42.8%	---	4.5%	2.5%	2.0%
Other prof service	169.6	67.1%	57.4%	22.4%	35.1%	9.7%	32.9%	24.4%	8.5%
Home health care	63.6	15.8%	11.5%	6.9%	4.6%	4.2%	84.2%	60.0%	24.2%
Drugs/non-durables	256.2	83.8%	83.8%	66.2%	17.6%	---	16.2%	8.6%	7.6%
Vision products/other medical durables	44.0	71.2%	71.2%	62.6%	8.5%	---	28.8%	26.3%	2.5%
Nursing home care	310.1	48.2%	46.3%	45.2%	1.1%	1.9%	51.8%	31.3%	20.5%
Oth personal hlth care	109.4	10.1%	---	---	---	10.1%	89.9%	53.1%	36.8%
Program admin & net cost of private health insurance	179.6	80.1%	78.6%	---	78.6%	1.5%	19.9%	12.3%	7.6%
Government public health activities	70.1	---	---	---	---	---	100%	12.7%	87.3%
Research and construction	80.4	30.4%	---	---	---	30.4%	69.6%	58.2%	11.4%

Table 64 (continued)									
Type of expenditure	Total	Private					Government		
2020 ($7,839.4 billion)		All Private	Consumer Total	Out of Pocket	Private Insurance	Other	Total	Federal	State & local
National health expenditure	$7,839.4	48.2%	44.6%	16.4%	28.2%	3.5%	51.8%	39.2%	12.6%
Health services/supplies	7,690.3	48.5%	45.5%	16.7%	28.8%	3.0%	51.5%	38.9%	12.6%
Personal health care	7,200.2	47.6%	44.5%	17.9%	26.6%	3.1%	52.4%	40.7%	11.7%
Hospital care	3,267.5	38.2%	33.5%	4.2%	29.3%	4.7%	61.8%	48.7%	13.1%
Physician service	1,861.6	49.9%	49.9%	15.0%	34.8%	0.0%	50.1%	43.9%	6.2%
Dental services	171.1	95.5%	95.5%	53.1%	42.4%	---	4.5%	2.5%	2.0%
Other prof service	335.2	66.6%	56.9%	22.2%	34.8%	9.6%	33.4%	24.9%	8.5%
Home health care	127.4	12.2%	8.9%	5.2%	3.7%	3.3%	87.8%	63.4%	24.4%
Drugs/non-durables	522.0	85.7%	85.7%	66.1%	19.6%	---	14.3%	7.5%	6.8%
Vision products/other medical durables	75.5	68.0%	68.0%	59.8%	8.2%	---	32.0%	29.6%	2.4%
Nursing home care	639.2	51.3%	49.3%	48.1%	1.2%	2.1%	48.7%	29.4%	19.3%
Oth personal hlth care	200.7	11.4%	---	---	---	11.4%	88.6%	52.3%	36.3%
Program admin & net cost of private health insurance	370.0	81.6%	80.1%	---	80.1%	1.5%	18.4%	11.3%	7.1%
Government public health activities	120.2	---	---	---	---	---	100%	12.5%	87.5%
Research and construction	149.1	30.9%	---	---	---	30.9%	69.1%	57.8%	11.3%

Source: Burner, S.T., Waldo, D.R., & McKusick, D.R. (1992). National health expenditures projections through 2030, Health Care Financing Review (14): 1, pp 1-29.

Table 64 (continued)									
Type of expenditure	Total	Private					Government		
2030 ($15,969.6 billion)		All Private	Consumer			Other	Total	Federal	State & local
			Total	Out of Pocket	Private Insurance				
National health expenditure	$15,969.6	48.5%	45.0%	17.1%	27.9%	3.5%	51.5%	39.6%	11.9%
Hlth services/supplies	15,691.8	48.8%	45.8%	17.4%	28.4%	3.0%	51.2%	39.3%	11.9%
Personal health care	14,753,7	47.9%	44.7%	18.5%	26.2%	3.2%	52.1%	41.1%	11.1%
Hospital care	6,680.8	38.3%	33.6%	4.5%	29.1%	4.7%	61.7%	49.6%	12.1%
Physician service	3,845.0	50.1%	50.1%	15.7%	34.4%	0.0%	49.9%	43.9%	6.0%
Dental services	279.7	95.7%	95.7%	53.7%	42.0%	---	4.3%	2.4%	1.9%
Other prof service	649.0	66.4%	56.8%	22.1%	34.7%	9.6%	33.6%	25.1%	8.5%
Home health care	287.5	13.5%	9.8%	5.5%	4.3%	3.6%	86.5%	62.2%	24.4%
Drugs/non-durables	1,045.3	87.4%	87.4%	66.2%	21.2%	---	12.6%	6.5%	6.1%
Vision products/other medical durables	127.4	64.4%	64.4%	56.7%	7.7%	---	35.6%	33.3%	2.3%
Nursing home care	1,477.4	53.8%	51.7%	50.4%	1.3%	2.2%	46.2%	27.8%	18.4%
Oth personal hlth care	361.6	13.1%	---	---	---	13.1%	86.9%	51.5%	35.4%
Program admin & net cost of private health insurance	732.1	82.1%	80.6%	---	80.6%	1.5%	17.9%	10.9%	7.0%
Government public health activities	206.0	---	---	---	---	---	100%	12.3%	87.7%
Research and construction	277.8	32.5%	---	---	---	32.5%	67.5%	56.4%	11.1%

Source: Burner, S.T., Waldo, D.R., & McKusick, D.R. (1992). National health expenditures projections through 2030, Health Care Financing Review (14): 1, pp. 1-29

Table 65: Elderly Long-Term Care Expenditure by Source of Payment: 1995

Source of payment	Amount	Percent
Nursing Home care:		
Medicaid	$ 24.2 billion	37.6%
Medicare	8.4	13.0%
Other Federal	0.7	1.1%
Other State and local	0.6	0.9%
Out-of-pocket payments	30.0	46.6%
Private insurance	0.4	0.6%
Total	64.4	
Home and community-based care:		
Medicaid	4.3	16.2%
Medicare	14.3	54.0%
Other Federal	1.7	6.4%
Other State and local	0.5	1.9%
Out-of-pocket payments	5.5	20.8%
Private insurance	0.3	1.1%
Total	26.5	

Source: U.S. House of Representatives. (1998). Committee on Ways and Means. 1998 Green Book.

Table 66: The Projection of Medicare and Medicaid Expenditures by type: United States, 1990-2030

Type of expenditure	1990		2000		2010		2020		2030	
	Medicare	Medicaid	Medicare	Medicaid	Medicare	Medicaid	Medicare	Medicaid	Medicare	Medicaid
(in billions)										
Hlth service/supplies	$111.2	$ 75.2	$327.6	$359.8	$862.9	$744.8	$1,950.0	$1,442.4	$4,133.9	$2,856.2
Personal health care	108.9	71.3	323.3	348.6	855.3	721.6	1,936.3	1,397.6	4,109.5	2,767.5
Hospital care	68.3	28.5	191.0	162.1	470.3	339.6	1,078.9	677.0	2,328.3	1,333.9
Physician services	30.0	5.2	104.1	24.9	324.3	53.5	733.9	99.9	1,533.5	179.0
Dental services	---	0.7	---	2.5	---	4.4	---	7.1	---	11.1
Other prof services	3.1	2.0	9.0	12.5	21.9	27.8	45.0	55.2	88.4	106.6
Home health care	2.9	2.2	9.0	15.8	20.2	33.3	44.2	67.4	96.3	151.9
Drugs/non-durables	---	4.9	---	19.5	---	36.9	---	65.1	---	111.7
Vision/other medical durables	2.2	---	5.8	---	10.9	---	21.3	---	40.7	---
Nursing home care	2.5	24.1	4.4	72.1	7.7	146.5	13.1	283.8	22.3	625.4
Oth personal hlthcare	---	3.6	---	39.2	---	79.7	---	142.1	---	247.9
Program admin	2.3	3.8	4.3	11.2	7.6	23.2	13.7	44.8	24.4	88.6
(% nat'l expenditure)										
Health	17.3	11.7	19.3	21.2	23.3	20.1	25.4	18.8	26.3	18.2
service/supplies	18.6	12.2	20.6	22.2	24.7	20.9	26.9	19.4	27.9	18.8
Personal health care	26.7	11.1	27.2	23.1	30.3	21.9	33.0	20.7	34.9	20.0
Hospital care	23.9	4.2	30.2	7.2	38.2	6.3	39.4	5.4	39.9	4.7
Physician services	---	2.2	---	4.0	---	4.2	---	4.1	---	4.0
Dental services	9.7	6.5	10.9	15.2	12.9	16.4	13.4	16.5	13.6	16.4
Other professional service	41.8	31.4	29.5	51.9	31.7	52.3	34.7	52.9	33.5	52.9
Home health care	---	9.1	---	15.6	---	14.4	---	12.5	---	10.7
Drugs/other medical non-durables	17.8	---	23.9	---	24.8	---	28.1	---	31.9	---
Vision products/other	4.7	45.4	3.0	49.0	2.5	47.2	2.1	44.4	1.5	42.3
medical durables	---	31.9	---	72.4	---	72.9	---	70.8	---	68.5
Nursing home care / Other personal health care	5.9	9.9	5.1	13.3	4.2	12.9	3.7	12.1	3.3	12.1
Program admin										
(% prog expenditure)										
Health	100%	100%	100%	100%	100%	100%	100%	100%	100%	100%
service/supplies	97.9	94.9	98.7	96.9	99.1	96.9	99.3	96.9	99.4	96.9
Personal health care	61.5	37.9	58.3	45.0	54.5	45.6	55.3	46.9	56.3	46.7
Hospital care	27.0	7.0	31.8	6.9	37.6	7.2	37.6	6.9	37.1	6.3
Physician services	---	1.0	---	0.7	---	0.6	---	0.5	---	0.4
Dental services	2.8	2.7	2.7	3.5	2.5	3.7	2.3	3.8	2.1	3.7
Other professional service	2.6	2.9	2.8	4.4	2.3	4.5	2.3	4.7	2.3	5.3
Home health care	---	6.6	---	5.4	---	5.0	---	4.5	---	3.9
Drugs/other medical non-durables	1.9	---	1.8	---	1.3	---	1.1	---	1.0	---
Vision products/other	2.2	32.1	1.3	20.0	0.9	19.7	0.7	19.7	0.5	21.9
medical durables	---	4.8	---	10.9	---	10.7	---	9.9	---	8.7
Nursing home care / Other personal health care	2.1	5.1	1.3	3.1	0.9	3.1	0.7	3.1	0.6	3.1
Program admin										

Source: Burner, S.T., Waldo, D.R., & McKusick, D.R. (1992). National health expenditures projections through 2030, Health Care Financing Review (14): 1, pp. 1-29

Informal Support

Table 67: Characteristics of Caregivers in Hawai`i (State Government Employee)

Characteristics	Number	Percentage
Age		
18 to 24	57	.7
25 to 34	1,027	13.5
35 to 44	2,657	34.9
45 to 54	2,808	36.9
55 to 64	914	12.0
65 or older	85	1.1
no data	66	.9
Average age 44.4 years old		
Sex		
Male	2,355	30.9
Female	5,144	67.6
no data	113	1.5
Income		
Less than $ 10,000	47	.6
$ 10,000 to $ 19,999	349	4.6
$ 29,000 to $ 29,999	688	9.0
$ 30,000 to $ 39,999	1,112	14.6
$ 40,000 to $ 49,999	1,328	17.5
$ 50,000 to $ 75,000	2,591	34.0
More than $ 75,000	1,319	17.3
no data	179	2.4
Median income $ 50,745		

Source: Hawai`i Executive Office on Aging (1990). Caring for Elderly Family Members: The Impact on Employed Caregivers. A Report on a Survey of State Government Employees Who are Caregivers to Older Adults.

Formal Support

Table 68: Summary of Available Formal Support Services in Hawai`i

Type of service	Total Facility (Agency)	Total Capacity	County	Number of Facility	Number of Capacity
Adult Day Care Center	16	563	O`ahu	10	235
			Kaua`i	3	72
			Maui	2	99
			Hawai`i	2	157
Adult Day Health Center/Day Hospital	6	119	O`ahu	3	80
			Kaua`i	0	0
			Maui	1	24
			Hawai`i	1	15
Adult Residential Homes (Both type I and II)	508	2609	O`ahu	407	2143
			Kaua`i	27	138
			Maui	27	127
			Hawai`i	47	201
Long-Term Care Facility (ICF) 1998*	4	459	O`ahu	1	218
			Kaua`i	1	36
			Maui	2	248
			Hawai`i	0	0
Long-Term Care Facility (SNF) 1998*	28	436	O`ahu	19	300
			Kaua`i	1	24
			Maui	0	0
			Hawai`i	8	70
Long-Term Care Facility (SNF/ICF) 1998*	36	3,021	O`ahu	18	2010
			Kaua`i	4	229
			Maui	6	362
			Hawai`i	8	608

Source: 1. The HMSA Foundation. (1999). Health Trends in Hawai`i: A Profile of the Health Care System.
　　　　　　Fourth Edition.
　　　　2. State Health Planning & Development Agency (1999). Long-term care List 1998. Honolulu, HI.
Note:　 * Facilities have been counted more than once depending on the type of services they provide.

Table 69: Hawai`i Licensed Health Care Providers by County 1997 (per 10,000 population)

Health Care Provider	Statewide	Hawai`i	Honolulu	Maui	Kaua`i
Dental Hygienists	4.1	3.0	4.3	5.1	2.5
Dentists	8.7	6.7	9.5	6.2	7.6
Physicians	25.6	17.4	28.4	18.7	17.5
Podiatrists	0.2	0.3	0.2	0.3	0.2
LPNs	21.9	25.7	20.0	22.4	39.5
RNs	81.8	69.2	85.9	72.8	68.8
Optometrists	1.8	0.9	2.0	1.3	1.4
Osteopaths	0.7	0.9	0.7	0.7	0.5
Pharmacists	6.5	5.2	6.9	5.2	6.4
Physical Therapists	3.6	4.2	3.5	4.3	3.2
Psychologists	3.0	2.8	3.2	2.4	1.4

Source: The HMSA Foundation (1999). Health Trends in Hawai`i: A Profile of Hawai`i Health Care System. Fourth Edition.

Table 70: Nursing Staff per Inpatient Bed of Long-Term Care Facilities in 1995: U.S. vs. Hawai`i
(Figure 23)

	RNs	LPNs	Nurse Aides
U.S.	0.10	0.15	0.41
Hawai`i	0.11	0.09	0.44

Source: Healthcare Association of Hawai`i (1997). Hawai`i Long-term care Facility Data Trends, 1991-1995

REFERENCES AND OTHER READINGS

Administration on Aging. (1996-a). <u>Estimates and Projection of the Older Population, by Age Group 1990-2050</u>, Retrieved August 13, 1999 from Web <u>www.aoa.dhhs.gov/aoa/stats/proj1tbl.html.</u>

Administration on Aging. (1996-b). <u>Aging Into the 21st Century</u>. National Aging Information Center May 31, 1996. Retrieved October 20, 1999 from the Web <u>www.aoa.gov/aoa/stats/aging21/default.htm.</u>

Anzick, M. (1993). Demographic and employment shifts: Implications for benefits and economic security. <u>EBRI Issue Brief</u> (140), 1-22.

Alwin, D. F. (1998). The political impact of the baby boom: Are there persistent generational differences in political beliefs and behavior? <u>Generations</u> 12 (1), 46-54.

Baker, K. K. et. al. (1998). <u>Multi-Race Health Statistics: A State Perspective Hawai`i Health Survey (HHS) 1998.</u> National Conference for Health Statistics. Retrieved January 17, 2000 from the Web: <u>www.Hawai`i.gov/health/stats/surveys/nchs.htm.</u>

Bartlett, D. F. (1999). The new health care consumer. <u>Journal of Health Care Financing</u> 25 (3), 44-51.

Bernheim, D. B. (1997). <u>The 1996 Merrill Lynch Baby Boom Retirement Index</u>. Retrieved July 24, 1997 from the Web <u>www.merrill-lynch.ml.com/personal/retire/bb_index.htlm.</u>

Blanchette, P. L. & Valcour, V. G. (1998). Health and aging among baby boomers. <u>Generations</u> 12 (1), 76-80.

Boomers give health care failing grade. (1998). <u>Patient-Focused Care and Satisfaction</u> 6 (5), 57-59.

Bouvier, L.F. & DeVita, C. J. (1991). The baby boom: Entering midlife., <u>Population Bulletin</u> 46(3). Washington, DC: Population Reference Bureau, Inc.

Browne, I. (1995). The baby boom and trends in poverty, 1967-1987. <u>Social Forces</u> 73 (3), 1071-1095.

Burke, G. (1993). Changing health needs of the elderly demand new policies. <u>Journal of American Health Policy</u> 3 (5), 22-26.

Burner, S.T., Waldo, D. R., & McKusick, D. R. (1992). National health expenditures projection through 2030. <u>Health Care Financing Review</u> 14 (1),1-29.

Butler, R. N. (1990). Will the baby boomers go bust? [editorial]. <u>Geriatrics</u> 45 (12),13-14.

Butler, R. N. (1994). Baby boomers: Aging population at risk [editorial]. <u>Geriatrics</u> 49(2),13-14.

Callahan, D. (1994). Setting limits: A response. <u>Gerontologist</u> 34 (3), 393-398.

Chernoff, R. (1995). Baby boomers come of age: Nutrition in the 21st century. <u>Journal of the American Dietician Association</u> 95 (6), 650-654.

Cornman J. M. & Kingson, E. R. (1996). Trends, issues, perspectives, and values for the aging of the baby boom cohorts. <u>Gerontologist</u> 36(1), 15-26.

Cornman, J. M. et al. (1997). Questions for societies with "third age" populations. <u>Academic Medicine</u> 72 (10), 856-862.

Cunningham, R. (1998). Perspectives: Solution gap looms for financing baby boomers' future long-term care needs. <u>Medicine & Health</u> 52 (12 Suppl.), 1-4.

Clydesdate, T. T. (1997). Family behaviors among early U.S. baby boomers: Exploring the effects of religion and income change, 1965-1982. <u>Social Forces</u> 76 (2), 605-635.

Crispell, D.(1995). Generations to 2025. <u>American Demographics</u> 17 (1), 4.

Davidhizar, R. & Giger-Newman, J. (1996). Reflections on the minority elderly in health care. <u>Hospital Topics</u> 74 (3), 20-24.

Dychtwald, K. (1997). The 10 physical, social, spiritual, economic and political crises the boomers will face as they age in the 21st century. <u>Critical Issues in Aging</u> (1):11-13.

Easterlin, R. A., Macdonald, C., & Macunovich, D. J. (1990). Retirement prospects of the baby boom generation: A different perspective. <u>Gerontologist</u> 30 (6), 776-783.

Frank-Stromborg, M. (1991). Changing demographics in the United States: Implications for health professionals. <u>Cancer</u> 67 (6 Suppl.), 1772-1778.

Friedland, R. B. & Summer, L. (1999). <u>Demography is not destiny</u>, Washington, DC: National Academy on an Aging Society

Fronstin, P. & Copeland, C. (1997). Medicare on life support: Will it survive? <u>EBRI Issue Brief</u> (189) 1-22.

Fullerton, H. N., Jr. (1991). Labor force projections: The baby boom moves on. <u>Monthly Labor Review</u> 114 (11), 31-44.

Ghiselli, W. B. & Frances, P. S. (1985). The impact of the baby boom on the mental health system. Hospital and Community Psychiatry 36 (5), 536-537.

Gist, J. R., Wu, K. B., & Ford, C. (1999). Do baby boomers save and, if so, what for? Executive summary. American Association of Retired Person (AARP). Retrieved January 29, 2000 from the Web www.research.aarp.org/econ/9906_do_boomers_1.html.

Gutheil, I. A. (1996). Introduction: The many faces of aging: Challenges for the future. Gerontologist 36 (1), 13-14.

Hardy, M. A. & Kruse, K. S. (1998). Realigning retirement income: The politics of growth. Generations 12 (1), 22-28.

Hawai`i Department of Economic and Business Development and Tourism. (1987). The State of Hawai`i Data Book 1987: A Statistical Abstract, Honolulu, HI.

Hawai`i Department of Economic and Business Development and Tourism. (1991). The State of Hawai`i Data Book 1991: A Statistical Abstract, Honolulu, HI.

Hawai`i Department of Economic and Business Development and Tourism. (1993). 1990 Census of Population and Housing, Hawai`i Data Disc, 1990 Population and Housing Summary Tape File 3A.

Hawai`i Department of Business and Economic Development and Tourism. (1996). Hawai`i's Economy Third Quarter Report, Honolulu, HI.

Hawai`i Department of Business, Economic Development, and Tourism. (1997-a). The State of Hawai`i Data Book 1997: A Statistical Abstract Honolulu, HI.

Hawai`i Department of Business, Economic Development, and Tourism. (1997-b). Population and Economic Projections for the State of Hawai`i to 2020: DBEDT 2020 Series. Report of Results and Methodology, Honolulu, HI.

Hawai`i Department of Business and Economic Development and Tourism. (1998). The State of Hawai`i Data Book 1998: A Statistical Abstract. Retrieved January 24, 2000 from the Web: www.state.hi.us./dbedt/

Hawai`i Department of Health. (1950). Annual Report-1950. Honolulu, HI.

Hawai`i Department of Health (1960). Statistical Report. Honolulu, HI.

Hawai`i Department of Health. (1970). Statistical Report. Honolulu, HI.

Hawai`i Department of Health. (1980). <u>Statistical Report</u>. Honolulu, HI.

Hawai`i Department of Health. (1990). <u>Annual Report, Statistical Supplement</u>. Honolulu, HI.

Hawai`i Department of Health. (1995). <u>Statistical Report</u>. Honolulu, HI.

Hawai`i Department of Health. (1996). <u>Vital Statistics</u>. Honolulu, HI.

Hawai`i Department of Health. (1997). <u>Health and Vital Statistics</u>. Retrieved January 25, 2000 from the Web: http://Hawai`i.gov

Hawai`i Department of Health. (1998). <u>Uninsured Population of Hawai`i, HHS 1998, Gender, Age, and Race</u>. Retrieved December 20, 1999 from the Web www.state/hi.us/doh/stats/surveys/hs_hsp.html.

Hawai`i Department of Health. (1999). <u>1996-1998 Hawai`i Behavioral Risk Factor Surveillance System Results</u>. Health Surveys and Disease Registry Section, Office of Health Status Monitoring. Honolulu, HI..

Hawai`i Department of Housing. (1999). <u>Hawai`i Housing Policy Study-1997 Update</u>. Retrieved January 25, 2000 from the Web www.hcdch.state.hi.us/hsgstats.html.

Hawai`i Department of Labor and Industrial Relations. (1999). <u>Selected Fast Growing Occupations, 1996-2006.</u> Retrieved January 30, 2000 from the Web: www.state/hi.us/dir/rs/loihi

Hawai`i Executive Office on Aging. (1990). <u>Caring for Elderly Family Members: The Impact on Employed Caregivers.</u> A Report on a Survey of State Government Employees Who are Caregivers to Older Adults. Honolulu, HI.

Hawai`i Executive Office on Aging (1991). <u>Financing Long Term Care: A Report to the Hawai`i State Legislature</u>. Honolulu, HI

Hawai`i Executive Office on Aging (1992). <u>Aging in Hawai`i: An Environmental Scan</u>. Honolulu, HI.:Author

Hawai`i Executive Office on Aging (1996). <u>2011 Project Briefing Book</u>. Honolulu, HI.:Author

Hawai`i Executive Office on Aging (1997). <u>Hawai`i's Older Adults</u>. Honolulu, HI.:Author

Hawai`i Executive Office on Aging (1998-a). <u>The Hawai`i Data Book for Older Adults</u>. Honolulu, HI.:Author

Hawai`i Executive Office on Aging (1998-b). <u>Hawai`i summit: Project 2011, A Strategic Plan for Action</u> Honolulu, HI.: Author

Hawai`i Executive Office on Aging (1999). <u>Project 2011: Baby Boomers and Retirement: Challenges and Opportunities.</u> Honolulu, HI: Karl Kim and Dolores Foley

Hawai`i State Health Planning & Development Agency. (1999). <u>Long-Term Care List 1998.</u> Honolulu, HI.: Author

Hawai`i Office of Hawaiian Affair. (1997). <u>Native Hawaiian Data Book, 1997</u>

Hawai`i Office of Hawaiian Affair. (1998). <u>Native Hawaiian Data Book, 1998</u>

Health Care Financing Administration. (1998). <u>HCFA Statistics: Highlights.</u> Retrieved February 10, 2000 from the Web www.hcfa.gov/stats/hstats98/highli98.htm.

Healthcare Association of Hawai`i. (1997). <u>Hawai`i Long-term care Facility Data Trends 1991-1995.</u> Honolulu, HI.: Author

Health care cost seen soaring as baby boomers age. (1993). <u>Health Care Financing Review</u> 14 (3), 305-306.

Helms, R. B. (1992). Implications of population growth on prevalence of diabetes. <u>Diabetes Care</u> 15 Suppl 1, 6-9.

Hooper, Susan. (2000, February 19). Inflation Rise on Mainland Narrows Gap on Living Costs. <u>The Honolulu Advertiser</u>, A1.

Jacobson, J. M. (1993). Midlife baby boom women compared with their older counterparts in midlife. <u>Health Care for Women International</u> 14 (5), 427-436.

Jordan Institute for Families. (1997). <u>Baby Boomers at Mid-Life: The Future of Aging in North Carolina.</u> A Report Prepared for the NC Division of Aging by Center for Aging Research and Educational Services, School of Social Work, the University of North Carolina at Chapel Hill.

Koenig, H. G., George, L. K., & Schneider, R. (1994). Mental health care for older adults in the year 2020: A dangerous and avoided topic. <u>Gerontologist</u> 34 (5), 674-679.

Kutza, E. A. (1998). A look at national policy and the baby boom generation. <u>Generations</u> 12 (1), 16-21.

Leventhal, R. C. (1994). The changing face of consumption: The aging of the baby boomers. <u>Journal of Hospital Marketing</u> 9(1),129-135.

Loke, M. (2000, February). [note sent by Matthew Loke of Med-Quest, Hawai`i Department of Human Services] Hawai`i Medicaid's Aged, Blind and Disabled Expenditure for SFY 1993-1998.

Longino, C. F. Jr. (1998). Geographic mobility and the baby boom. Generations 12 (1), 60-64.

Lumsdon, K. (1993). Baby boomers grow up. Hospitals & Health Networks 67 (18), 24-26, 28-34.

Lusky, R. A. (1986). Anticipating the needs of the U.S. aged in the 21st century: Dilemmas in epidemiology, gerontology, and public policy. Social Science Medicine 23 (12), 1217-1227

Macunovich, D. J., Easterlin, R. A., Schaeffer, C. M., & Crimmins, E.M. (1995). Echoes of the baby boom and bust: Recent and prospective changes in living alone among elderly widows in the United States. Demography 32 (1), 17-28

Manton, K. G. & Stallard, E. (1996). Changes in health, mortality, and disability and their impact on long-term care needs. Journal of Aging & Social Policy 7 (3-4), 25-52

Marosy, J. P. (1997). Elder caregiving in the 21st century. Caring 16 (5), 14,16,18-21

Minnesota Department of Human Services. (1997). Aging Initiative: Project 2030

Montana Department of Public Health and Human Services, Senior and Long-term care Division (1998). The State of Aging in Montana:The Aging Baby Boom: Implications for State Government. Helena, MT: Author.

Morgan, D. L. (1998). Facts and figures about the baby boom. Generations 12(1):10-15

New initiative provides best practices for elderly. (1998). Healthcare Benchmarks 5(2), 24-25

Pillemer, K. & Suitor, J. J. (1998). Baby boom families: Relations with aging parents. Generations 12 (1), 65-69

Poulos, S. & Nightingale, D. S. (1997). The aging baby boom: Implications for employment and training programs (Contract No. F-5532-5-00-80-30). Washington, D.C.: The Urban Institute.

Pretzer, M. (1997). Getting Medicare ready for the baby boomers. Medical Economics 74(21): 35, 40, 43

Rice, D. P. (1996). Beneficiary profile: Yesterday, today, and tomorrow. Health Care Financing Review 18(2): 23-45

Roper Starch Worldwide, Inc. (1999). Baby boomers envision their retirement: An AARP segmentation analysis, executive summary. American Association of Retired Persons.

Scablon, W. J. (1998). Future financing of long-term care. Consumer's Research Magazine 81(6):16-20

Scanlon, W. (1998). Long-term care: Baby boom generation presents financing challenges. Testimony before the Special Committee on Aging, U.S. Senate, United States General Accounting Office, GAO/T-HEHS-98-107

Siegel, J. (1996). Aging into the 21st century. National Aging Information Center, Administration on Aging, U.S. Department of Health and Human Services. HHS100-95-0017

Silverstone, B. (1996). Older people of tomorrow: A Psychosocial profile. The Gerontologist 36(1):27-32

Singer, B. H. & Manton, K. G. (1998). The effects of health changes on projections of health service needs for the elderly population of the United States. Proc. Natl. Acad. Sci. 95:15618-15622

The HMSA Foundation. (1999). Health trends in Hawai`i: A profile of the health care system Honolulu, HI.

The Robert Wood Johnson Foundation. (1996). Chronic Care in America: A 21st Century Challenge. Princeton, New Jersey.

Treas, J. (1995). Older Americans in the 1990s and beyond. Population Bulletin 50(2) Population Reference Bureau, Inc. Washington, D.C.

U.S. Census Bureau (1992). 1990 Census of Population. General Population Characteristics Hawai`i, Series CP-1-13

U.S. Bureau of Census. (1993-a). Race by Educational Attainment. 1990 Census of Population and Housing Summary Tape File 3A.

U.S. Bureau of Census. (1993-b). Marital Status and Living Arrangement: March 1993, Current Population Reports. Retrieved January 25, 1999 from the Web www.census.gov/prod/1/pop/p23-190/p23190-1.pdf

U.S. Bureau of Census. (1996-a). Population and Housing Characteristics of Baby Boomers 26-44 years old: 1990. Retrieved October 18, 1999 from the Web www.census.gov/population/censusdata/cph-1-160h.txt.

U.S. Bureau of Census. (1996-b). <u>Selected Social Characteristics of Baby Boomers 26-44 years old: 1990</u>. Retrieved October 18, 1999 from the Web www.census.gov/population/censusdata/cph-1-160h.txt.

U.S. Bureau of Census (1998-a). <u>State Population Estimates 1998</u>. Retrieved October 25, 1999 from the Web www.census.gov/population/estimates/state/stats/ag9898.txt

U.S. Bureau of Census. (1998-b). <u>Statistical Abstract of the United States 1998: The National Data Book.</u> U.S. Department of Commerce, Economics, and Statistics Administration. Washington, D.C.

U.S. Bureau of Census. (1999-a). <u>Estimated Median Age at First Marriage, by Sex: 1890 to the Present</u>. Release date: January 7, 1999. Retrieved January 30, 2000 from the Web www.census.gov/populatiom/socdemo/ms_la/tabms_2.txt.

U.S. Bureau of Census. (1999-b). <u>Current Population Survey</u>, generated by Harumi Karel; Ferret; <u>Www.census.gov/des/pl:</u> (29, January 2000)

U.S. Bureau of Census. (1999-c). <u>Population Projection</u>. Retrieved January 20, 2000 from the Web www.census.gov/population/www/projection/nat.det-D1a.html.

U.S. Bureau of Census. (1999-d). <u>Marital Status for States, by sex for the population 15 years old and over: 1990 Census</u>. Retrieved February 10, 2000 from the Web www.census.gov/population/socdemo/ms_la/tabms.st1.txt.

U.S. Census Bureau. (1999-e). <u>Health Insurance Coverage: 1998.</u> Retrieved October 15, 1999 from the Web: <u>www.census.gov.</u>

U.S. Department of Commerce. (1960). Bureau of Census. 1960 Census of Population. Volume 1. <u>Characteristics of the Population Part 13.</u> Hawai`i.

U.S. Department of Health and Human Services (1996). National Center for Chronic Disease Prevention and Health Promotion. <u>Behavioral Surveillance Branch. Behavioral Risk Factor Surveillance System 1984- 1995 Survey Data.</u> CD-ROM Series 1, No.1 2nd Edition.

U.S. Department of Health and Human Services. Center for Disease Control and Prevention. (1997). <u>BRFSS</u>. Retrieved January 25, 2000 from the Web: www.cdc.gov/nccdphp/brfss/index.asp.

U.S. Department of Health and Human Services. (1999). National Center for Disease Control and Prevention. <u>BRFSS</u>. Retrieved January 25, 2000 from the Web www2.cdc.gov/nccdphp/brfss/index.asp.

U.S. House of Representatives, Committee on Ways and Means. (1998). <u>1998 Green Book.</u>. Washington, DC: GPO 1998

U.S. Senate. (1991). <u>Long-term care: Projected needs of the aging baby boom generation</u>. Report to the Honorable William S. Cohen, Special Committee on Aging, Washington, DC: General Accounting Office, [1991] GAO HRD 91-86

U.S. Senate. (1997). <u>2010 and beyond: Preparing Medicare for the baby boomers</u>. Hearing before the Special Committee on Aging, United States Senate, One Hundred Fifth Congress, first session, Sioux, City, IA, August 25, 1997. Washington, DC: GPO CSO 115:105-229

U.S. Senate. (1998). <u>Preparing for the retirement of the baby boom generation</u>. Hearing before the Special Committee on Aging, United States Senate, One Hundred Fifth Congress, second session, Baton Rouge, LA,, February 18, 1998. Washington, DC: GPO Y4.Ag4:S.HRG.105-471

Vatter, R. H. (1993). Demographic trends from an economist's point of view. <u>Statistical Bulletin Metropolitan Insurance Co.</u> 74(4):27-32

Vatter, R. H. (1998). Boomers enter the golden fifties. <u>Statistical Bulletin Metropolitan Insurance Co.</u> 79(1):2-9

Vincenzino, J. V. (1996). Household savings in the United States: Trends and outlook. <u>Statistical Bulletin Metropolitan Insurance Co.</u> 77(1):21-7

Wattenberg, E. (1986), The fate of baby boomers and their children. <u>Social Work</u> 31(1): 20-28

Well, J. (1996). Baby boomer needs will spur growth of long-term care plans. <u>Compensation and Benefits Review</u> 28(2):49-53

Williamson, J. B. (1998). Political activism and the aging of the baby boom. <u>Generations</u> 12(1):55-59

Yakoboski, P. & Silverman, C. (1994). Baby boomers in retirement: What are their prospects? <u>EBRI Issue Brief</u> (151): 1-42

Yung-Ping Chen (1999). Racial Disparity in Retirement Income Security: Directions for Policy Reform. In Toni P. Miles (Ed.), <u>Full-Color Aging: Facts, Goals, and Recommendations for America's Diverse Elders</u> (pp.21-31). Washington, DC: The Gerontological Society of America.